DATE DUE

4-26-07			

Demco

Online Newswriting

Online Newswriting

K. Tim Wulfemeyer

 **Blackwell** Publishing

K. TIM WULFEMEYER is a Professor in the Journalism Degree Program, School of Communication, San Diego State University. He has extensive radio-TV news experience, both on-the-air and behind the scenes as writer, reporter, producer, photojournalist, newscaster and sportscaster for radio and television stations in California, Iowa, New Mexico, Texas and Hawaii.

Blackwell Publishing Professional
2121 State Avenue, Ames, Iowa 50014, USA
Orders: 1-800-862-6657
Office: 1-515-292-0140
Fax: 1-515-292-3348
Web site: www.blackwellprofessional.com

Blackwell Publishing Ltd
9600 Garsington Road, Oxford OX4 2DQ, UK
Tel.: +44 (0)1865 776868

Blackwell Publishing Asia
550 Swanston Street, Carlton, Victoria 3053, Australia
Tel.: +61 (0)3 8359 1011

First edition, 2006

Library of Congress Cataloging-in-Publication Data

Wulfemeyer, K. Tim.
  Online newswriting / K. Tim Wulfemeyer.—1st ed.
    p. cm.
  ISBN-13: 978-0-8138-0049-3 (alk. paper)
  ISBN-10: 0-8138-0049-8 (alk. paper)
  1. Online journalism.   2. Journalism—Authorship.   I. Title.

PN4784.O62W85 2006
808.06607—dc22   2005034902

The last digit is the print number: 9 8 7 6 5 4 3 2 1

Table of Contents

Introduction

Writing news for web sites on the Internet is a bit different from writing news for a traditional newspaper, magazine, radio station or television station. Good writing is good writing, of course, but the style and tone of online newswriting sets it apart from its older news media brothers and sisters.

Effective online newswriting is really a hybrid of the best of print news media writing and radio-television newswriting. The mechanics of online newswriting borrow heavily from newspapers and magazines, but the flow and tone of online newswriting follow the more conversational aspects of radio-television newswriting. The best online newswriting is much like online "chatting." The style is a bit less informal, but the tone is very similar.

The important thing, as in all newswriting, is to tell a good story. Tell it concisely, accurately, fairly, interestingly and entertainingly. It's not an easy task, but it can be a very satisfying and rewarding task, if you do it well. Most experts agree that the ability to write news online will be critical for most, if not all, journalists. Most good schools and departments of journalism at colleges and universities require that their students receive training and practice in writing for print, radio-television and online news media.

If you're not already reading news online on a regular basis, start visiting at least one web site of a newspaper, magazine, radio station or television station every day. You'll see some good examples and some not-so-good examples of online newswriting. Be sure to incorporate the good examples into your own writing and avoid the mistakes you encounter. Being familiar with the various models of online newswriting will help you get more out of reading this book and will help you do your best work on the writing assignments in the book.

Visit http://www.assignmenteditor.com and the web sites of your local newspapers, radio stations and television stations. Surf around. Check out the links. Explore. Learn.

In *Online Newswriting*, we'll cover the basic mechanics, flow, style, tone, methods and techniques of online newswriting. In addition, we'll cover some of the many legal and ethical concerns that confront online news writers on a regular basis.

Online Newswriting builds on traditional introductions to basic newswriting. It is assumed that you already will have had an introductory newswriting or writing for the mass media course or that you are using this book as part of such a course. Many fundamental elements of quality newswriting for any medium are included in this book, but the emphasis is on quality online newswriting.

Writing is the focus of *Online Newswriting*. We will not cover the creation of graphics, page layout or the technical aspects of web sites. Such visual and technical elements are important partners with the creation of text for web sites, but they are beyond the scope of this book.

Online Newswriting is divided into five sections. In the first section, you'll be introduced to many of the theoretical, philosophical and practical aspects of writing online news. In the second section, you'll be introduced to concerns associated with incorporating pictures, graphics, audio and video elements into your online news stories. In the third section, you'll be introduced to a variety of general tips for more effective online newswriting. In the fourth section, you'll be introduced to some of the major legal and ethical concerns associated with online newswriting. Finally, in the fifth section, you'll be given opportunities to practice what you've learned about online newswriting. You'll get a chance to demonstrate how much you know about online newswriting style and you'll be asked to rewrite news briefs and full stories from simulated wire copy, news releases, reporters' notes and fact sheets from various organizations.

Throughout *Online Newswriting*, you'll be given opportunities to think and write about the suggestions for improving your writing. You'll be able to comment on the models provided. You'll be able to see how well you've understood the guidelines and examples. Take the time to think and write each time you're given the opportunity. The Write About It sections will enhance your learning from and enjoyment of *Online Newswriting*.

Unless your instructor tells you differently, whenever you write a story from information contained in this book, you have to imagine that you're working for a news organization in the mythical city of Midcity. Midcity is located in a Midwestern state in the United States. It could be similar to Des Moines, Iowa. It could be similar to Columbus, Ohio. It could be similar to Indianapolis, Indiana.

ABOUT MIDCITY

Here are some basic facts about Midcity.

Population:	978,642
Top Executive Officer:	Mayor Ronald R. Moore
Legislative Body:	Nine-member Board of Supervisors
Court System:	Municipal Courts: civil cases involving amounts of no more $5,000 and all criminal cases where the possible term of incarceration is one year or less. These criminal cases are called misdemeanors, petty misdemeanors and violations.
	Superior Courts: civil cases involving amounts of more than $5,000 and all criminal cases where the possible term of incarceration is more than one year. These criminal cases are called felonies.
Schools (public):	Midcity Unified School District. Grades kindergarten through high school. Enrollment: 179,752
Higher Education (public):	Midcity University. Offers B.S./B.A., M.S./M.A., Ed.D., Ph.D., J.D., M.D., D.V.M. Enrollment: 28,500
	Midcity Community College. Offers A.S./A.A. Serves people interested in vocational training and people preparing to transfer to four-year colleges and universities. Enrollment: 10,790

ACKNOWLEDGMENTS

Special thanks to the following for their contributions to the creation of *Online Newswriting*:

Lori Wulfemeyer, assistant dean, Thomas Jefferson School of Law

Jim Holtzman, Jim Holtzman Productions

Chris Jennewein, *San Diego Union-Tribune*

Cliff Albert, Clear Channel Communications

Robert Ponting, KNSD-TV, San Diego

Thanks also to the many students at Iowa State University, New Mexico State University, the University of Hawaii and San Diego State University, who served as unknowing test subjects and who contributed many of the examples used in this book.

Online Newswriting

SECTION ONE

Theories, Philosophy, Style, Methods and Techniques

Quality online newswriting is timely, informative, entertaining, clear, concise, accurate, balanced and fair. Among the advantages that online newswriting enjoys over its competing media are the ability to update and freshen copy on a more-or-less continual basis; the opportunity to include audio, video, graphics and photos; the ability to go into greater depth and provide important background information associated with issues and events; and the ability to help readers gather information on their own by providing links to other web sites, documents and databases.

Creating compelling, engaging, interesting and entertaining copy is critical when writing news online. Audio, video, photos, graphics and the ability to provide links to more information are important "extras" that can be used to enhance the impact of news copy, but the text itself must attract and hold readers. All of the bells and whistles of interactivity, movement, sound and color that can be found on many web sites goes for naught if the copy falls flat.

Effective online newswriting comes in many styles, shapes and sizes. Just as in the more traditional journalistic media, ownership, locale and audience characteristics play important roles in determining what style and tone your writing should take.

In *Online Newswriting*, you'll be encouraged to develop and use a basic style of online newswriting that would be appropriate for the web sites of traditional news media organizations. Keep in mind, though, that there are many non-traditional news sites on the World Wide Web that feature irreverent, hip-hop, no-holds-barred, "tabloidish" styles of writing.

CHATTING UP READERS

Online newswriting should be conversational. It should read much like the copy used in radio and television news. It should be similar to how people write when they're "chatting" with family and friends online.

Strive for a "telling a story" tone. Pretend that you're telling a story to a friend. Use simple words. Use colorful words. Use words that paint clear mental pictures for readers. Avoid the stilted, formal, convoluted style of writing that sometimes can be found in the print media and in technical manuals.

Use simple, declarative sentences. The subject-verb-object format works well. Limit your use of phrases and clauses. Assume you're writing for someone who is about 12 years old. This doesn't mean you have to "dumb down" your copy. It just means that you should attempt to write clearly, directly and in a manner that is easy for readers to understand and remember what you're telling them. Readers are busy. They turn to web sites for quick, easy to comprehend information. Give it to them.

You can be informal and still inform. You can be conversational and still impress. You can tell a story to readers and still touch them and/or make a difference in their lives. You don't have to write in a pedantic, preaching manner to appear intelligent and authoritative. Your job is to communicate with people who have busy lives and a great deal on their minds. Make it easy for them to read your copy. Make it easy for them to understand your copy. Make it easy for them to enjoy your copy. Make them want to revisit your web site often to obtain the information they want and need.

Example:

• Seniors Scam

Authorities have announced the arrest of a former San Diego-area Insurance agent accused of scamming senior citizens out of $1.7 million over a two-year period. Glenn Martin III, 57, is charged with swindling seniors into attending bogus investment seminars and duping them into investing in fake promissory notes that never paid out.

Martin, who was arrested last Thursday, is charged with 29 counts of grand theft, financial elder abuse, making a false statement in the sale of securities and tax evasion. "Senior citizens are especially vulnerable to get-rich-quick schemes and dishonest sales tactics when unscrupulous agents outright lie about investment opportunities," said state Insurance Commissioner John Garamendi, "Taking advantage of a person's retirement funds is as despicable as it gets, and my department will continue to aggressively pursue, investigate and help prosecute individuals who seek to rip off our most vulnerable citizens' hard-earned savings," Garamendi said.

Martin's alleged scams materialized as the promissory notes came due and victims came forward to file formal complaints with the San Diego County District Attorney's Office. Martin allegedly used the "bogus" seminars and solicitations to dupe seniors into investing their money in the various schemes between 2001 and 2003. Seniors were told they could get 20 to 24 percent returns on their investments, District Attorney Bonnie Dumanis said. "This con man preyed on of the most vulnerable segments of society to support his lavish lifestyle," she said. "The California Department of Insurance and the Franchise Tax Board will join with our office to see that this predator is brought to justice.

Martin has pleaded not guilty to the charges and is being held in lieu of $500,000 bail pending an Oct. 11 preliminary hearing.

Example:

State Officials Push For Tsunami Preparedness Funds

POSTED: 10:45 am PDT July 25, 2005

LOS ANGELES -- State lawmakers are appealing for federal funds to increase tsunami preparedness in Southern California.

June 2005 Images: Tsunami Warning
Image Gallery: Dec. 2004 Asian Tsunami

NBC in Los Angeles said 85 percent of tsunamis are triggered in the Pacific Ocean, and a "dozen or so" have been triggered in the last 100 years. Now that the Tsunami Preparedness Act has passed the U.S. House and is awaiting U.S. Senate approval, local agencies say federal funds could help Californians react if a tsunami hit.

An official of the California Tsunami Safety Committee told NBC that a Southern California tsunami generated by a landslide off Palos Verdes could be as big as 42 feet tall and 25 miles wide. The committee is meeting Monday morning in Manhattan Beach, Calif.

Coastal areas are equipped with loud speakers and air raid sirens, but officials told Kovacik they would also like to have an automatic system that would notify coastal dwellers and boaters with a text message or phone call.

Sen. Barbara Boxer (D-Calif.) is pushing for such warning systems, saying they would minimize casualties.

"The thing would be horrific but it would not be catastrophic," Boxer said.

More complete warning systems would also include escape routes and signage warning people of tsunami disaster, Kovacik reported.

The Carson City tsunami warning six weeks ago triggered teletypes from an Alaska tsunami warning center, and those warnings reached local law enforcement agencies in six minutes, reported NBC.

Now officials are looking for ways to get the word out quickly to the general population.

Example:

Police pursuit ends in plunge into ravine

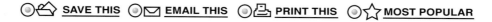
⊙🔖 **SAVE THIS**   ⊙✉ **EMAIL THIS**   ⊙🖨 **PRINT THIS**   ⊙☆ **MOST POPULAR**

UNION-TRIBUNE BREAKING NEWS TEAM

7:33 a.m. July 27, 2005

ESCONDIDO - A man tried to elude police in a stolen car Tuesday night, only to end up taking the fall - about 75 feet down a ravine.

An officer tried to stop the car for a traffic violation shortly before 11 p.m. at Valley Center Road and Lake Wohlford Road, but the driver wouldn't pull over, instead continuing northeast on winding Lake Wohlford Road, Escondido police said.

A few minutes later the driver stopped the car on the steep grade and ran, then jumped over a concrete barrier alongside the road, only to tumble down a steep embankment, police said said.

The man landed on some rocks at the bottom of the hill and firefighters had to rappel down the slope to reach him. He was treated at a hospital before being taken to jail.

"He didn't break anything, but he was bruised up pretty good," said police Sgt. Paul Woodward.

A passenger remained with the car and was taken into custody without a struggle. The car, a Hyundai sedan, turned out to be stolen, Woodward said.

The driver was booked into County Jail on suspicion of possession of a stolen vehicle and felony evading arrest. Woodward said the passenger also was booked, for a parole violation.

■ Greg Gross: (619) 293-1889; greg.gross@uniontrib.com

Example:

Rescuers Free Man Pinned Beneath Mobile Home

POSTED: 3:23 pm PDT July 25, 2005
UPDATED: 4:19 pm PDT July 25, 2005

SAN DIEGO -- A construction worker had a very close call Monday when a trailer home fell on him, pinning him.

 IMAGES: Man Pinned By Mobile Home

"It sounded like something big fell, and then he started screaming," said neighbor Ashley Noonan.

Frank Torres and three other construction workers were setting up a new doublewide trailer at the Lamplighter Mobile Home Park in Lakeside when something slipped.

"The house wasn't level," said construction worker Derek Young. "We were trying to jack it up straight, and it fell over. Probably jack failure, I would guess"

The mobile home landed on Torres' lower leg. Young, who told NBC 7/39 that he estimates the trailer weighs 35,000 pounds, and he stayed with Torres until help arrived.

"I was talking with him, holding his hand, you know, to make sure he was conscious and coherent," said Young. "He was breathing -- he wasn't going into shock or anything. He was just screaming bloody murder...."

Firefighters used special inflatable bags and a device that operates like the Jaws of Life to lift the house and free Torres. They told NBC 7/39 that the equipment was purchased two months ago with a special grant. With it, they were able to extricate the victim in just 21 minutes. Without it, they said, it would have taken a lot longer.

Young said that nothing like this had ever happened while he was working.

"It was pretty random," said Young.

KEEP IT SHORT AND SWEET

Even though length is essentially irrelevant when writing news online, more often than not you'll be asked to keep your stories relatively short. Most people don't like to have to scroll through page after page of dense copy on a small computer screen. Just as in writing for radio or television news, get to the point of your story quickly, tell a good story and provide enough valuable information to help readers keep up with what's happening in their hometown, region, state, nation and world.

Example:

● New School Supt

 Carl Cohn, who received national attention for turning around the Long Beach school system, will become San Diego's new superintendent of City Schools. The San Diego school board was expected to make the announcement at a news conference, putting an end to a superintendent search process that began when Alan Bersin was forced out.

Richard Loveall, director of executive search services for the California School Boards Association, told the Union Tribune, "They have one of the top superintendents in the nation by anybody's standards, who is a proven commodity for years and years."

Under Cohn's leadership, the Long Beach Unified School District was recognized as one of the best urban districts nationwide for having made dramatic improvements in student performance, attendance and behavior. The 97,000-student district was the first in the nation to require school uniforms for students in kindergarten through eighth grade. During his tenure, from 1992 to 2002, student absenteeism and suspensions dropped significantly.

Example:

Small Quakes Keep Shaking California

POSTED: 6:39 pm PDT July 24, 2005
UPDATED: 6:44 pm PDT July 24,2005

OXNARD, Calif. -- A medium-size earthquake hit off the coast of Ventura County early Sunday.

No damages or injuries have been reported.

The U.S. Geological Survey said the 4.2-magnitude temblor hit at about 6 a.m. about 28 miles southeast of Santa Rosa Island and 51 miles southwestt of Oxnard.

On Saturday, a small earthquake shook Lake County near Santa Rosa.

The 3.2-magnitude quake struck at 5:31 a.m. in The Geysers and about 24 miles north of Santa Rosa, according to preliminary reports from the U.S. Geological Survey.

There were no reports of damage or injury, a Lake County dispatch operator said.

Several minor quakes have struck off the coast or in California since a major quake off the coast of Northern California triggered a Tsunami warning on June 14.

Example:

Police: Woman Used Web To Sell Dogs That Don't Exist

Suspect Accused Of Selling Dogs That Don't Exist

POSTED: 1:36 pm PDT July 22, 2005
UPDATED: 3:31 pm PDT July 22, 2005

SAN DIEGO -- Police in Chula Vista arrested a woman this week who they say was running an Internet pet scam selling pets that didn't exist.

 IMAGES: Internet Pet Scam

Elizabeth Rivera Davis was taken into custody by officers in Chula Vista on Wednesday. She faces 17 felony burglary charges and 17 felony counts of theft by fraud, all felonies.

According to law enforcement in Chula Vista, Rivera Davis conned customers of her fake Internet pet store into buying purebred terriers that did not exist. Police said she had buyers from around the United States, some of whom paid as much as $800 for the animal.

In fact, say police, the only dog Rivera Davis owns is not even a terrier.

Officials said Rivera Davis told at least 20 "buyers" since December 2004 they would receive their animals after they sent money to her through Western Union. Police said Rivera Davis changed her online and mailing addresses during the course of the scam.

Police were finally able to collar Rivera Davis, they said, after they learned she was using a Chula Vista Western Union where she did, in fact, use her real name.

Chula Vista law enforcement believes Rivera Davis may have had other "customers" they have yet to identify. Any one who suspects they might have been a victim of Rivera Davis should call the Chula Vista Police Department at (619) 409 5487.

At her arraignment Friday, Rivera Davis pleaded not guilty to all charges. She is being held on $175,000 bail.

Example:

• Internet Pet Scam

Authorities say Elizabeth Rivera Davis started and operated an Internet pet store where she claimed to sell purebred terriers of all types. Dog lovers from across the country responded to her ads and some sent upwards of $800 to her via Western Union, with the promise the dogs would be then be delivered, CVPD reported.

Police say the only problem was that Davis never shipped a dog. The only dog she has is a family dog, and it's not the breed she was claiming to sell. Davis did this over 20 times to different people across the country. She would change her e-mail address and mailing address each time, CVPD reported.

Detectives learned Davis was using a Western Union storefront in Chula Vista to receive her payment, and there she used her correct name and cell phone number. This information was all that stayed consistent. The addresses she listed were to places like empty lots and the library, CVPD reported. Investigators learned she has been doing this at least since last December. A warrent was issued for her e-mail service, as well as her phone.

Davis was arrested by the Chula Vista Police Department on Wednesday July 20 and charged with 17 counts of burglary and 17 counts of theft by fraud, all felonies. She is scheduled to be arraigned on Friday July 22 at 1:30 p.m. in department 16 of the South Bay Courthouse. The alleged victims ordered dogs from as far away as the east coast and Canada. Police say there are probably more victims that police are not yet aware of.

If you believe you are a victim of this scam, contact Detective Tom Halfaker at (619) 409-5487.

Example:

Police: Nevada Kidnapping Suspect In San Diego

POSTED: 5:56 pm PDT July 24, 2005
UPDATED: 8:30 am PDT July 25, 2005

SAN DEIGO -- An Amber alert has been issued in California for a young girl who may have been kidnapped in Nevada by a convicted sex offender.

Fernando Aguero and Lydia Rupp

Police are looking for Fernando Aguero, the boyfriend of the little girl's mother, who is believed to be in San Diego with the girl.

"We are relatively convinced that he is in the San Diego area," said Lyon County (Nev.) sheriff's Capt. Jeff Page. "We're flooding the area, (with publicity) pretty hard."

Investigators believe Aguero kidnapped 8-year-old Lydia Bethany-Rose Rupp and her dog while the mother was at work. They're believed to be in a silver or blue Kia sedan with a temporary dealer's tag in the rear window.

The girl is Latina, 4 feet 9 inches tall and weighs 85 pounds. She has brown hair and eyes and a dog-bite scar on her cheek.

Aguero, 47, is Latino, about 5 feet 10 inches and 150 pounds, with brown eyes and graying black hair. He was born in Tijuana, and police believe he crossed the border with the girl in the San Diego area. The California Highway Patrol told the *San Diego Union-Tribune* that the Amber alert remains in effect because investigators believe Aguero is moving back and forth between Mexico and San Diego County.

Aguero was released from prison 10 years ago for committing a lewd and lascivious act upon a child under 14 in Los Angeles, Page said.

If you see the car, the girl or the suspect you're asked to contact the California Highway Patrol.

Example:

● Amber Alert

There is new information in the search for an 8-year-old Nevada girl believe to have been kidnapped Friday by a convicted sex offender. Investigators said the two may have travelled through San Diego County.

The new lead comes from the mother of the accused kidnapper. She lives in Reno but told Nevada deputies that her son has been spotted with Lydia Rupp by relatives in Tijuana. The local FBI is now working with Mexican authorities to find the girl and bring her home. "We do have conversation and dialogue with Mexican law enforcement about Lydia, and we do have reason to believe that she's in Mexico with the subject and we're working closely with them," Jan Caldwell, with the FBI, said. San Diego law enforcement has been on high alert for the girl since cell phone calls linked the suspect to the local area. The California Highway Patrol focused this weekend on highways near downtown and near the border.

"We had information that he may actually been in the car. Officers were looking for the vehicle, circling the parking lots near the border, if need be, and various areas around the country," Mark Gregg, with the CHP said. But the mother of Fernando Aguerro said he may have already taken the girl to Tijuana, where the two were spotted by relatives. Aguerro is the boyfriend of Rupp's mother. He moved in shortly after the two met at this church, 10News reported. The pastor said he didn't trust the newcomer. "I don't know much about him, so when he came to tell me he wants to minister, I said no," pastor Matt McCreary said.

Investigators said Aguerro dropped the girl's mother at work on Friday and then took Rupp from their home -- even grabbing her clothes, pictures, birth certificate and dog. A Nevada sheriff's captain said Aguerro was convicted of lewd and lascivious acts upon a child under 14 in Los Angeles in 1985. He served one year behind bars, but when he moved to Nevada, he didn't register as a sex offender. Investigators are hoping he'll simply let Rupp go. Rupp has a 10-year-old brother, but he was not harmed.

The amber Alert was still on for two reasons -- the lead may not pan out and it's possible Aguerro is driving back and forth to the U.S. Rupp is Latina, has brown hair, brown eyes, and scars on her cheeks. She weighs 85 pounds and is 4 feet 9 inches tall. Aguero, a Latino, has silver-grey hair, a moustache, scars on both arms, and a large scar on his lower right leg and foot. The CHP said Aguero was last seen in San Diego county driving a bluish silver 2001 Kia Rio with paper plates that say Reno Mazda Kia.

Anyone who sees the pair is urged to 911 or the Lyon County, Nevada, Sheriff's Office at (775) 463-6620.

Example:

Ramp to I-8 reopens following 3-vehicle crash

⊙🖾 **SAVE THIS**   ⊙✉ **EMAIL THIS**   ⊙🖨 **PRINT THIS**   ⊙☆ **MOST POPULAR**

UNION-TRIBUNE BREAKING NEWS TEAM

August 2, 2005

SAN DIEGO - A collision Tuesday morning between a Honda sedan, a Ford Expedition SUV and a commercial water-delivery truck closed the northbound ramp from Interstate 805 to westbound Interstate 8 for more than half an hour, the California Highway Patrol reported.

■ **Live: Traffic map**

The crash occurred shortly before 8 a.m. Emergency units intitially had trouble getting through backed-up traffic to reach the crash site, but they were able to reopen the ramp after about 40 minutes, said CHP Officer Jim Bettencourt.

No injuries were reported.

Example:

Man Admits Murdering Publisher 18 Years Ago

POSTED : 8:52 am PDT July 28, 2005
UPDATED: 9:25 am PDT July 28, 2005

SAN DIEGO -- A 39-year-old man has pleaded guilty to first-degree murder in the slaying of a San Diego newspaper publisher.

 IMAGES: 1987 Murder Scene

Stanley Clayton acknowledged killing William Thompson, 61, in his Emerald Hills home in 1987. Thomson was publisher of the Voice and Viewpoint newspaper.

The San Diego County District Attorney's office said Clayton will be sentenced to life in prison without the possibility of parole.

Clayton, a three-strikes felon, was serving a sentence of 35 years to life at Centinela State Prison in Imperial County on a burglary conviction when a match was made in a DNA database. San Diego Police detectives reopened the investigation in 2003.

Previous Stories:

- February 23, 2005: Convict Enters Plea In Journalist's 1987 Murder
- February 17, 2005: Suspect In 1987 Murder May Face Death Penalty

---

Example:

One Dead After Truck Slams Into Big Rig

POSTED: 8:15 am PDT July 26, 2005
UPDATED: 8:51 am PDT July 26, 2005

SAN DIEGO -- One person died Monday evening after two trucks collided on Interstate 15.

 IMAGES: Crash-Scene Photos

The crash occured at about 5:45 p.m. on I-15 near Mission Road. The smaller truck ran into a moving van, pinning itself underneath the larger truck.

The California Highway Patrol said it took two hours to get two victims out of the trapped truck. According to authorities, one of the people later died at the hospital. The other crash victim was taken to Palomar Hospital for treatment. The condition of the second victim is not being released.

Traffic backed up during the evening commute while rescuers worked to save the victim.

Example:

• Postal Employee Sentenced

A 33-year veteran of the U.S. Postal Service, who stole $430,311 in money orders from his employer over a three-year period, was sentenced Monday to 30 months in federal prison. Robert Franklin Lenz, 55, pleaded guilty April 25 to one count of theft of public money.

Lenz, a former postal manager, abused his power by taking advantage of a flaw in the Postal Service's system and directing clerks to deposit only part of the money orders in USPS accounts and returning the rest to him, authorities said. Assistant U.S. Attorney John J. Rice argued that Lenz took money in 80-90 incidents from December 2001 until December 2004. "I just screwed up," the Alpine resdent told U.S. District Judge Marilyn Hugg. "I let something like downsizing get to me. I bit the hand that helped me for 33 years."

BE AN ORIGINAL

Much of the online newswriting you do will be completely original, but when you're asked to rewrite wire copy, a news release, a reporter's notes, or a previously written story, be sure that you significantly change whatever source copy you've been given. Change the lead for sure. Change the order of information. Freshen and/or update information. Retell the story in YOUR words.

Analyze the source copy. Think about what additional information is needed. What's missing? What do readers want to know? What do readers need to know? Become a reporter. Make some calls. Conduct some interviews. Check some web sites. Ask co-workers. Supplement the source copy with newly acquired information. Give readers good reasons to check your web site often for the latest news, weather and sports.

Example:

• Heat Wave Cooling Off

An unusual thunderstorm with lightning, rain and thunder affected many areas of San Diego County this weekend as moisture from former Hurricane Emily combined with a high-pressure dome over the region according to the National Weather Service. Officials say there were more than 1500 lightning strikes, but there were no reports of any damage except for a couple of small brush fires. One brush fire burned about 100 acres in Proctor Valley. The storms prompted a flash flood watch in some mountain areas. Thunderstorm could still develop through Monday.

Most of the precipitation and lightning wil be over the desert and mountains, where temperatures should be lowered by moisture and cloud cover with a few inches of rain that could fall in some higher-elevation areas.

The current heat wave is being called the worst one in San Diego in ten years. Temperatures have been setting records throughout the county and humidity levels are unusually high from the coast to the mountains.

Lightning strikes sparked a series of small brush fires and that prompted state fire officials to officially declare a HIGH FIRE DANGER condition. People who are camping and picnicking are urged to be extra careful about campfires and matches.

Thousands of people sought refuge from the heat the San Diego beaches where the ocean water temperature is said to be in the low 70's in some areas. Lifeguards are out in force. SDG&E customers are asked to set their thermostats at 78 to 80 degrees and avoid using large appliances until after 7 p.m.

The County has information about ways to guard yourself from any heat-related problems. Click here for more.

Other Local Stories:
- New School Supt
- Mayoral Election Tuesday
- Seniors Scam
- Internet Pet Scam
- Prop "A" Need 2/3
- Councilmen Resign
- Daily War Report
- Gas Prices Up

KOGO COMMUNITY CALENDAR

Example:

Rare Jellyfish Invades Local Waters

Beachgoers Get Unpleasant Surprise

POSTED: 7:23 pm PDT July 26, 2005
UPDATED: 10:30 am PDT July 27, 2005

SAN DIEGO -- San Diego beachgoers are encountering a new danger in local waters. A rare type of jellyfish has been stinging dozens of swimmers a day in recent weeks, according to San Diego lifeguards.

IMAGES: Jellyfish Invasion
IMAGES: Giant Squid Return
IMAGES: Giant Squid Wash Ashore

Experts at Birch Aquarium say the giant black jellyfish is the reason for all the stings. They started showing up off the coast in late June, according to Vincent Levesque of the Birch Aquarium. Unlike purple striped jelly fish, which show up along the coast every year, the giant blacks have been spotted in local waters only five times in the last 80 years, Levesque said.

Levesque said it isn't clear why they are here, but onshore winds are probably pushing them into shallow water.

"It's almost impossible to nail it down to one defining thing, especially with the black jellies," Levesque said.

Lifeguards are seeing an increasing number of close -- and painful -- encounters between swimmers and the black jellyfish.

We're seeing probably 20 to 30 a day or more at busier stations," said Sgt. Jon Vipand of the San Diego Lifeguard Service.

It's definitely something you want to avoid, Vipand said. "Pretty painful. They don't require hospitalization, but they will raise welts on your hand."

A marine biologist with the California Department of Fish and Game said giant blacks aren't the only rare jellyfish in local waters. He said the fried egg jellyfish has also been spotted along the coast recently.

Previous Stories:

- March 22, 2005: North County Beach Awash In Squid
- March 16, 2005: More Jumbo Squid Beach Themselves
- January 20, 2005: Jumbo Squid Wash Up On SoCal Beaches

Example:

● Hit & Run Case

San Diego police are searching for the motorist responsible for a hit-and-run accident that killed a 19-year-old San Diego woman.

Angelina Padilla was walking east in the roadway on the south side of Clairemont Mesa Boulevard near Rolfe Road at about 1:20 a.m. Saturday when she was hit from behind, according to the San Diego Police Department. Padilla was taken to a hospital where she died from head trauma. Police believe the woman was walking home after having an argument with her boyfriend, The San Diego Union-Tribune reported.

According to police, Padilla was hit by a late-60s to mid-70s dark-colored Ford van, which fled without stopping. The vehicle has a square front end, no windows on the sides and may have windows on the back doors. Crime Stoppers is asking vehicle repair shops to be on the lookout for damage to the right-front headlight and/or parking light of vehicles matching the description of the suspect vehicle. Anyone with information on the accident is urged to call police at (858) 495-7800, or you can call Crime Stoppers' toll-free anonymous tip line at (888) 580-TIPS.

Crime Stoppers is offering up to a $1,000 reward to anyone with information that leads to the arrest of this suspect. Collect calls are accepted and callers may remain anonymous.

Example:

Cops Search For Teen Girl's Hit-And-Run Killer

POSTED: 11:52 am PDT July 26, 2005
UPDATED: 12:18 pm PDT July 26, 2005

SAN DIEGO -- Family and friends are mourning the death of a San Diego State University student and are hoping the hit-and-run driver who killed her will be captured.

 IMAGES: Teen Killed by Hit-And-Run Driver.

Flowers, cards and candles mark the site where a van struck and killed 19-year-old Angie Padilla. According to San Diego Police, Padilla was walking in a lane on Clairemont Mesa Boulevard when she was hit by a van.

Police said the driver never even slowed down.

A witness who saw the van driving away from the accident said was dark in color. Officials think the vehicle may be an older model Ford from the 1970s or '80s. The van has no rear windows on the sides, and the front of it is square in shape.

Police said the van will have damage to its right front end. Anybody with information about the killing is being urged to call the San Diego police.

Example:

Casino's Customers Urged To Get Tested For TB

POSTED: 8:53 am PDT July 27, 2005
UPDATED: 9:05 am PDT July 27, 2005

SAN DIEGO -- Health officials are warning visitors of Casino Pauma that they might have been exposed to tuberculosis.

According to the County Health Department, a patron was diagnosed with infectious tuberculosis earlier this year. Authorities are now urging partrons who visited the casino between Jan. 1 and May 7 to get a TB test. Health officials said only visitors who spent more than 120 hours at the casino should be tested.

The health department said that the person who was originally diagnosed with tuberculosis has been treated and is no longer a risk.

✉ Email This Story | 🖶 Print This Story

Example:

• Casino TB Scare

County health officials Tueday advised employees of a North County casino -- and those who frequented the business during the first four months of the year -- to get tested for tuberculosis.

Dr. Nancy Bowen, the county public health officer, said that a patron of Casino Pauma, 777 Pauma Reservation Road, was diagnosed and treated for infectious TB. " We recommend that those who visited the casino between Jan. 1 and May 7 and were there 120 hours or more, contact their physician and request an evaluation that includes a TB skin test," Bowen said. The casino will post signs with the warning, she said.

TB symptoms include a persistent cough, fever, night sweats and unexplained weight loss, Bowen said. However, most people exposed to TB do not contract the disease, she said. If you would like more information, call the county TB control branch at (619) 692-8621.

DEVELOPING AND EVOLVING NEWS

Online news is a prefect medium for reporting on developing and evolving issues and events. Take advantage of the ability to update and to branch out to cover each and every angle associated with the main focus of your story.

Take a look at how a special election was covered by the online journalists at KOGO-AM, KNSD-TV and the *San Diego Union-Tribune*. The stories are good examples of how online news media can provide clear, concise, yet thorough coverage of important issues and events.

Example:

• Mayoral Election Tuesday

Early voting is now available in Tuesday's special San Diego Mayoral election. The Registrar of Voters Office on Ruffin Road is open for early voting from 8am-to 5pm.

The six major candidates are coming down to the wire in their campaigns to become the next San Diego Mayor. The election will be held Tuesday, July 26th, with the polls open from 7am to 8pm.

A majority winner in the election would serve out the duration of the term of Mayor Dick Murphy who resigned this month. If no candidate receives more that 50 percent of the vote, there will be a runoff election.

Listen for LIVE coverage and election results starting at 8 o'clock Tuesday night.

The mayoral ballot will include these candidates:
-- Councilwoman Donna Frye;
-- Jerry Danders, former San Diego police chief;
-- Steve Francis, a businessman;
-- Richard Rider, a Libertarian and chair of San Diego Tax Fighters;
-- Pat Shea, an attorney;
-- Mike Shelby, a motocycle dealership owner;
-- Jim Bell, an ecological designer;
-- Shawn McMillan, a businessman and attorney;
-- Jeremy Ledford, a businessman;
-- Ed Kolker, a mediator and arbitrator; and
-- Tom Knapp, a restaurant supervisor.

Click here for City Clerk elections info.

Example:

Mayoral Hopefuls Stick To Scripts In Final Debate
Voters Go To Polls On Tuesday

POSTED: 6:56 am PDT July 25, 2005
UPDATED: 7:40 am PDT July 25, 2005

SAN DIEGO -- With one day left before San Diegans go to the polls to elect a new mayor, a new poll shows a tight race for second place.

⊕ Enlarge

Donna Frye, Steve Francis and Jerry Sanders

The most recent Datamar Survey shows Councilwoman Donna Frye still in front with the support of 46 percent of the voters surveyed. But unless she manages to capture more than 50 percent of the votes cast Tuesday, she will face a runoff with the second-place candidate.

The race for second place is a satistical dead heat, according to the Datamar poll. Millionaire businessman Steve Francis, with 22 percent support, is just ahead of former Police Chief Jerry Sanders, who polled 21 percent. Francis, who has spent well over $1 million on television commercials, has steadily gained in the weekly polls. His rise has been largely at Sanders' expense. In the first Datamar poll, Sanders had the support of more than 30 percent of the voters polled.

The six top canditates appeared Sunday evening on the second of two debates broadcast by NBC 7/39. Front-runner Frye looked relaxed and said she was glad this part of the campaign is almost over. Asked about saving the city's financial crisis, Frye didn't rule out a possible tax increase or bankruptcy. But she said voters would always have the last word.

"No matter what is on the table, as far as any kind of increases, it would always go to a vote of the public," Frye said.

Francis again promised no new taxes. Instead, he promised to solve the city's financial problems by cutting spending.

"Instead of an 8 to 10 percent cut, it may be a 15 to 20 percent reduction," he said. "There is only so much money available. It's going to come out of the government."

Sanders promised a strong leadership team at City Hall. He said he would work to include controversial City Attorney Mike Aguirre.

"I think that's the most critical part of this -- trying to fashion a way for Mike to feel like a part of this process. And I think that can be done with strong leadership," Sanders said.

Most of the candidates offered specific measures to flesh out their platforms, but attorney Pat Shea said he is being the clearest by spelling out his plan to restructure the city's finances through bankruptcy.

"I'm the only person who is running on a platform that the people absolutely know what I'm going to do on day one." Shea said.

Finally, polls show motorcycle shop owner Myke Shelby trailing the pack with single-digit support. But the New York transplant said he isn't throwing in the towel. As he did during last Sunday's debate, he tried to put San Diego's problems into perspective.

"There are some things wrong, but it's nowhere near like what goes on in Chicago, New York or New Jersey. Do you know how many people they indict in New Jersey each year? We had it once in a decade," he said, referring to last week's conviction of two city councilmen on corruption charges. "Who cares?"

Voters will decide who had the most effective message on Tuesday. NBC 7/39 and Ml San Diego TV43 will have reports on the vote count throughout the night Tuesday. Results will also be available all night on a live webcast on NBCSandiego.com.

Example:

S.D. voters to choose mayor, vote on cross

◉△ **SAVE THIS**   ◉✉ **EMAIL THIS**   ◉🖨 **PRINT THIS**   ◉☆ **MOST POPULAR**

UNION-TRIBUNE

July 26, 2005

It is Election Day in the city of San Diego, with residents voting to pick a new mayor and decide whether the federal government should take control of the Mount Soledad cross and war memorial.

Eleven candidates are vying to replace former Mayor Dick Murphy, who announced in April that he would resign July 15, eight months into his second term, amid a whirlwind of financial problems.

> ■ **Mayoral forum video and candidate profiles**
>
> SignOnSanDiego will have up-to-the-minute results and more election coverage tonight.

Councilwoman Donna Frye appears to have a firm grip on first place, according to multiple polls, with former Police Chief Jerry Sanders and business executive Steve Francis vying for second place and a ticket to join Frye in a possible Nov. 8 runoff.

Also on the ballot is Proposition A, a measure that calls for the city to donate the cross on La Jolla's Mount Soledad, the war memorial there and the land on which they sit to the U.S. Interior Department as a national veterans memorial.

Proposition A requires a two-thirds majority vote to pass.

Voters can cast ballots at the Registrar of Voters Office, 5201 Ruffin Road, Suite I, in Kearny Mesa or at one of the city's 713 polling places from 7 a.m. to 8 p.m.

Election-related questions will be answered by phone at (858) 565-5800, also from 7 a.m. to 8 p.m.

Voters can log on to **www.sdvote.com** to look up their polling places, view their sample ballot and find answers to other election-related questions.

The *San Diego Union-Tribune* would like to hear from voters who have problems at the polls. They can contact the paper at (800) 339-VOTE or (800) 339-8683.

Example:

Voters, Candidates Cast Special-Election Ballots

POSTED: 10:46 am PDT July 26, 2005
UPDATED: 12:00 pm PDT July 26, 2005

SAN DIEGO -- Voters -- and candidates -- in San Diego on Tuesday faced a mayoral ballot for the second time in less than nine months.

NBCSandiego.com's Wall-to Wall LIVESTREAM Election Coverage Begins At 8 P.M.
Decision 2005: Special Election
Find Your Polling Place

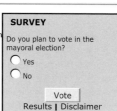

SURVEY

Do you plan to vote in the mayoral election?

○ Yes

○ No

Vote
Results | Disclaimer

The leading candidate was maverick City Councilwoman Donna Frye, who narrowly lost a write-in bid to replace Mayor Dick Murphy last year when a judge tossed out thousands of ballots because voters who wrote her name down failed to darken the adjoining bubble.

If the 53-year-old surf shop owner and registered Democrat finishes first but falls short of a majority, she would compete in a Nov. 8 runoff against her closest rival.

Two Republicans -- Steve Francis and Jerry Sanders -- appeared to be dueling for second place among the 11 hopefuls going into Tuesday's balloting.

Frye cast her vote at a little after 8 a.m. on Tueday at Clairemont Covenant Church in Clairemont, while Sanders voted about a half-hour earlier at the Kensington Church Hall in Kensington. Francis, meanwhile, voted Monday by absentee ballot.

"I feel good," Frye told NBC 7/39. "We've worked hard. We have people out today and all morning actually, going out, talking to voters, and dropping off reminders to vote, get out the vote, so we've got, you know, thousands of volunteers on the street, and I feel good."

Sanders, too, commented about the efforts of his campaign's volunteers.

"I feel very confident," said Sanders. " Volunteers have worked very hard, I've worked hard, my family has worked extremely hard. We're just happy to have voting day here. It's going to be a lot of fun."

Francis, 50, was a political unknown in San Diego until he spent about $2 million on a campaign that promoted himself as a businessman and outsider. He founded hospital staffing company AMN Healthcare Inc. after a stint in the Nevada state legislature in the 1980s.

"I really feel we have the wind at our backs." Francis said after casting his absentee vote Monday at the county Registrar's office. "We've come from virtually nowhere in the polls to, some would say, dead even ... wth Jerry Sanders."

The 55-year-old Sanders has cast himself as a turnaround specialist, touting his record as police chief from 1993 to 1999 and positions at the local United Way and American Red Cross chapters.

Murphy, a Republican and former judge, announced soon after this re-election that he planned to resign, saying he wanted to give San Diego a fresh start after the disputed election and amid a widening federal investigation of the city's pension fund.

Less than 72 hours after Murphy left office July 15, his interim replacement, Deputy Mayor and City Councilman Michael Zuccent, lost the job when a jury convicted him of federal corruption charges in a failed scheme to overturn San Diego's ban on touching dancers at strip clubs.

Frye and her remaining colleagues named Councilwoman Toni Atkins interim mayor until a replacement is elected.

At 10 a.m., NBC 7/39 said there were no reports from the registrar's office of any voting problems, though when Frye voted, she did have to fill in her bubble twice because she folded her ballot. Election workers tore up the folded ballot and had Frye fill out a replacement, which did go through.

Example:

• Frye vs Sanders; Prop A Wins

San Diego Councilwoman Donna Frye, who failed in a controversial write-in compaign to defeat Mayor Dick Murphy last fall, will face former police chief Jerry Sanders in a mayoral run-off election in November to finish out the mayoral term of Murphy who resigned July 15th.

In Tuesday's special mayoral primary election, Frye finished in 1st place among eleven candidates with 43-percent of the vore. Sanders finished 2nd with 27 percent while business owner Steve Francis finished 3rd with 24 percent of the vote. Pat Shea was 4th, Richard Rider 5th and Myke Shelby 6th followed by five minor candidates.

Proposition A, the measure to keep the War Memorial Cross on Mt. Soledad by turning it over to the federal government's park service, was approved by a huge margin of 76-to-24-percent. Just five days before the election, a local judge ruled that Prop A would have to get two-thirds approval instead of just a majority, but it passed easily anyway.

MAYOR - UNEXPIRED TERM

721 of 721 precincts - 100.0 percent
DONNA FRYE 104872 43.32%
JERRY SANDERS 65399 27.01%
STEVE FRANCIS 56887 23.50%
PAT SHEA 5720 2.36%
RICHARD RIDER 3756 1.55%
MYKE SHELBY 3533 1.46%
SHAWN A. MCMILLAN 561 0.23%
JIM BELL 473 0.20%
ED KOLKER 415 0.17%
JEREMY LEDFORD 378 0.16%
THOMAS KNAPP 98 0.04%

PROP A - Mt. Soledad Veteran Memorial Property (REQ 2/3)

721 and 721 precincts - 100.0 percent
YES 179820 75.90%
NO 57107 24.10%

Example:

Measure To Preserve Cross Passes Easily

Proposition A May Face Court Challenge

POSTED: 11:55 pm PDT July 26, 2005
UPDATED: 8:42 am PDT July 27, 2005

SAN DIEGO -- San Diego voters Tuesday approved a measure seeking to preserve the 29-foot-tall cross on city-owned land on Mount Soledad.

 **IMAGES:** Soledad Cross
Election Results

Proposition A passed easily even though a judge ruled last week that it needed a two-thirds majority to pass. With 100 percent of the precincts reporting, the measure was supported by 76 percent of voters. It needed a little less than 67 percent support to pass.

The cross has been the subject of a 15-year legal battle over whether its presence on city parkland violated the separation of church and state.

Proposition A, which could face a court challenge, would transfer the cross and surrounding land to the federal government.

 Email This Story | Print This Story

DO THE MATH

Online news writers should use their common sense and critical-thinking abilities to evaluate the accuracy and reasonableness of source copy. If something doesn't seem right to you, check it out. Do some fact-checking. If you discover errors, correct them. Don't pass along inaccurate information just because it's in the source copy.

It's critical that online news writers DO THE MATH in connection with numbers and statistics. Check the addition, subtraction, multiplication and division. Be sure the numbers are accurate and make sense. If they don't, make the appropriate changes after consulting with the proper sources to clarify inconsistencies.

Example:

(source copy information) Aunt Sally's Bake Shoppe averages 10,000 customers a day and takes in an average of $5,000 per day.

If you divide $5,000 by 10,000 customers, you get an average of 50 cents per customer. Since nothing costs 50 cents or less at Aunt Sally's Bake Shoppe, something's not right. Perhaps the reporter misheard Aunt Sally, or Aunt Sally might have misspoke, or maybe Aunt Sally or the reporter transposed the numbers. Maybe it's really 5,000 customers and $10,000 per day. That would make more sense.

Whatever the reason, the original numbers don't make sense. You'd have to check with the reporter and Aunt Sally to clear up the mistake BEFORE sending out the information to unsuspecting readers. Never pass along inaccurate, nonsensical or misleading information. It would be better to hold the story for a while or simply leave out the customer/income information until you can get things clarified. Be a crusader for improving journalism. Don't contribute to the problem of lazy, careless, inferior journalism.

Write About It

List TEN tips for improving the quality of online newswriting.

1.

2.

3.

4.

5.

6.

7.

8.

9.

10.

MAKE IT INTERESTING

Think about what will interest your readers. What do they want to know? What do they need to know? What do they care about? What will impact them? What will touch them? What will make them think? What will make them want to visit your web site again?

Your job, in large part, is to make important events, issues and developments interesting and to make interesting events, issues and developments important. Strive to help people find meaning in their lives and the lives of others. Help people gain a better understanding of why individuals, groups and organizations believe what they believe, value what they value and do what they do.

Traditional news values and elements provide some insights into what interests readers. The values and elements include information that is significant, information that is timely, information that deals with well-known people, and information that deals with local people, issues and events. In addition, such things as conflict, oddity, humor, achievements, sex and romance, heroism, advice about how to do things and animals (especially if they do something unusual) seem to interest readers, too.

People are interested in money-related matters—costs, salaries, bids. They're interested in winners and losers, pros and cons, advantages and disadvantages, benefits, frequencies, procedures, rules, guidelines, parameters, processes, future plans, past accomplishments, historical perspectives, impacts, justifications, explanations, rationales, excuses, forecasts, speculations, analyses and perspectives.

Researchers have identified several reasons why people turn to news outlets for information. Among the major reasons are the following:

1. To keep up with what's happening in their local communities, region, state, nation and world

2. To be reassured that they are making the right decisions in their lives and to be reassured that other people have more problems than they do

3. To be exposed to the opinions of others and to compare their own opinions with the opinions of others

4. To be entertained, amused and diverted from the stresses and pressures of their lives

5. To relax, get excited, or "feel" some form of human emotion

5WS AND THE H

Journalists have long been encouraged to include information in their stories that answers six fundamental questions. These questions are:

1. WHO is involved?

2. WHAT has happened?

3. WHERE did it take place?

4. WHEN did it take place?

5. WHY did it happen?

6. HOW did it happen?

Online journalists should not be content with simply answering the six fundamental questions. There are many more who, what, where, when, why and how questions that need to be answered. Such questions include the following:

Who was involved?
Who will be involved?
Who could be involved?
Who should be involved?
Who is affected?
Who was affected?
Who will be affected?
Who pays?
Who has paid?
Who will pay?
Who benefits?
Who has benefited?
Who will benefit?
Who wins?
Who has won?
Who will win?
Who loses?
Who has lost?
Who will lose?
Who is at fault?
Who has been at fault?
Who will be at fault?
Who is guilty?
Who was guilty?
Who will be guilty?
Who is innocent?
Who was innocent?
Who will be innocent?
When has it happened?
When will it happen?
When could it happen?
When should it happen?
When will we know?
When should we know?
How should this happen?
How much?
How many?
How often?

What will happen?
What could happen?
What should happen?
What might have happened?
What is the significance?
What has been the significance?
What will be the significance?
What is affected?
What has been affected?
What will be affected?
What causes the situation?
What has caused the situation?
What will cause the situation?
What is being done?
What has been done?
What will be done?
What does it mean?
What has it meant?
What will it mean?
What is the result?
What has been the result?
What will be the result?
Where has it happened?
Where will it happen?
Where could it happen?
Where should it happen?
Where do we go from here?
Where could we go from here?
Why will it happen?
Why could it happen?
Why should it happen?
Why do people need to know?
Why will people care?
Why should people care?

Write About It

List TEN elements that you could include in your stories that likely would interest readers.

1.

2.

3.

4.

5.

6.

7.

8.

9.

10.

LINKS TO MORE INFORMATION

Links to additional information can be included in a variety of ways in online newswriting.

1. Web site addresses can be included at the end of stories.

2. Icons with such labels as "Learn More, Know More, For More Information, Additional Information, Archives" can be placed at the end of stories, in the margins or even embedded within the text.

3. Highlighted words or names can be used in the text to indicate links to additional information.

Example:

Carrie Sherman's eyes well up with tears when she talks about her son, Matthew, 24, a laid back young man with a great sense of humor. Matthew joined the Midcity Police Department five days ago. Three days ago, he was killed in a freak accident at the Midcity Gun Range. The police department uses the range for practice, training and certification.

The West Midcity mother has several unanswered questions about her son's death and she's been camping out in a park across from Mayor Ronald Moore's house. She vows to maintain her vigil until Moore agrees to talk to her.

"My son is dead and I want to know why," Sherman said. "Is that too much to ask? He was just beginning his life. There was no reason for him to die and I've got to make sure he didn't die for nothing. I don't want any other mother, wife or husband to go through what I'm going through."

Sherman, 53, says her son was not wearing a protective, bullet-proof vest during training exercises and she wants to know why. Matthew was killed when a gun was knocked from a shelf and discharged. The bullet pierced Matthew's heart.

Assistant Police Chief Dennis Ackerman met with Sherman this morning, but Sherman called the meeting "worthless."

Moore is out of town on city business and Sherman says she'll continue to camp out until the mayor can explain to her why he cut the police department's budget last month. The budget cuts lead to the cancellation of an order for protective vests for officers.

> http://www.mpd.gov
> http://www.midcitymayor.gov
> http://www.policevests.com

Example:

Carrie Sherman's eyes well up with tears when she talks about her son, Matthew, 24, a laid back young man with a great sense of humor. Matthew joined the Midcity Police Department five days ago. Three days ago, he was killed in a freak accident at the Midcity Gun Range. The police department uses the range for practice, training and certification.

The West Midcity mother has several unanswered questions about her son's death and she's been camping out in a park across from Mayor Ronald Moore's house. She vows to maintain her vigil until Moore agrees to talk to her.

"My son is dead and I want to know why," Sherman said. "Is that too much to ask? He was just beginning his life. There was no reason for him to die and I've got to make sure he didn't die for nothing. I don't want any other mother, wife or husband to go through what I'm going through."

Sherman, 53, says her son was not wearing a protective, bullet-proof vest during training exercises and she wants to know why. Matthew was killed when a gun was knocked from a shelf and discharged. The bullet pierced Matthew's heart.

Assistant Police Chief Dennis Ackerman met with Sherman this morning, but Sherman called the meeting "worthless."

Moore is out of town on city business and Sherman says she'll continue to camp out until the mayor can explain to her why he cut the police department's budget last month. The budget cuts lead to the cancellation of an order for protective vests for officers.

Learn More

Example:

Carrie Sherman's eyes well up with tears when she talks about her son, Matthew, 24, a laid back young man with a great sense of humor. Matthew joined the Midcity Police Department five days ago. Three days ago, he was killed in a freak accident at the Midcity Gun Range. The police department uses the range for practice, training and certification.

The West Midcity mother has several unanswered questions about her son's death and she's been camping out in a park across from Mayor Ronald Moore's house. She vows to maintain her vigil until Moore agrees to talk to her. **For More Information About Mayor Moore**

"My son is dead and I want to know why," Sherman said. "Is that too much to ask? He was just beginning his life. There was no reason for him to die and I've got to make sure he didn't die for nothing. I don't want any other mother, wife or husband to go through what I'm going through."

Sherman, 53, says her son was not wearing a protective, bullet-proof vest during training exercises and she wants to know why. Matthew was killed when a gun was knocked from a shelf and discharged. The bullet pierced Matthew's heart. **For More Information About Bullet-Proof Vests**

Assistant Police Chief Dennis Ackerman met with Sherman this morning, but Sherman called the meeting "worthless." **For More Information About Dennis Ackerman**

Moore is out of town on city business and Sherman says she'll continue to camp out until the mayor can explain to her why he cut the police department's budget last month. The budget cuts lead to the cancellation of an order for protective vests for officers.

Example:

Carrie Sherman's eyes well up with tears when she talks about her son, Matthew, 24, a laid back young man with a great sense of humor. Matthew joined the Midcity Police Department five days ago. Three days ago, he was killed in a freak accident at the Midcity Gun Range. The police department uses the range for practice, training and certification.

The West Midcity mother has several unanswered questions about her son's death and she's been camping out in a park across from **Mayor Ronald Moore**'s house. She vows to maintain her vigil until Moore agrees to talk to her.

"My son is dead and I want to know why," Sherman said. "Is that too much to ask? He was just beginning his life. There was no reason for him to die and I've got to make sure he didn't die for nothing. I don't want any other mother, wife or husband to go through what I'm going through."

Sherman, 53, says her son was not wearing a protective, **bullet-proof vest** during training exercises and she wants to know why. Matthew was killed when a gun was knocked from a shelf and discharged. The bullet pierced Matthew's heart.

Assistant Police Chief **Dennis Ackerman** met with Sherman this morning, but Sherman called the meeting "worthless."

Moore is out of town on city business and Sherman says she'll continue to camp out until the mayor can explain to her why he cut the police department's budget last month. The budget cuts lead to the cancellation of an order for protective vests for officers.

Write About It

List THREE methods of including links to additional information in your online news stories. Which method do you prefer? Why?

1.

2.

3.

Preferred Method:

Why?

VERBS

Try to use present-tense verbs whenever you can. They drive home the timeliness aspect of online journalism and improve the flow of the story. If a present-tense verb is not appropriate (too much time has passed since the event occurred), use a present-perfect tense verb. If that doesn't work, you can always use the past tense.

Don't feel compelled to use present-tense verbs, though. Sometimes they just don't make sense for the subject matter or the timetable involved. Always try to use a present-tense verb or a present-perfect-tense verb, but if it makes more sense and reads better to use the past tense, then use it.

Example: (present tense) Sen. Edward Whittler is running for governor.

Example: (present perfect tense) Sen. Edward Whittler has announced that he's running for governor.

Example: (past tense) Sen. Edward Whittler announced that he's running for governor.

Example: (present tense) A fire is burning out of control in West Midcity.

Example: (present perfect tense) A fire has burned more than 300 acres in West Midcity.

Example: (past tense) A fired burned more than 300 acres in West Midcity.

Try to keep verbs in the active voice rather than the passive voice. The active voice normally saves a few words and can lend a fresher, more timely feel to the copy. The active voice follows the subject-verb-object pattern of the declarative sentence.

The passive voice slows down copy, adds extra words and can make copy seem tiresome, especially if the passive voice is used several times in a single story. It generally reverses the subject-verb-object order and makes the object the subject and the subject the object of a prepositional phrase. You can recognize passive-voice constructions by the use of a past-tense, present-perfect-tense or past-perfect-tense verb. A prepositional phrase often is included, too.

It is relatively easy to create passive-voice sentences when you're writing under deadline pressure. Learn to recognize passive-voice sentences and at least try to turn them into active-voice sentences by taking the object of the preposition and making it the subject of the sentence. In addition, take the subject of the passive-voice sentence and make it the object.

Example: (passive voice) The fire was started by an electrical short circuit.

Example: (active voice) An electrical short circuit started the fire.

Example: (passive voice) The winning touchdown was scored by Terrell Mack.

Example: (active voice) Terrell Mack scored the winning touchdown.

Example: (passive voice) Midcity University has been given a $1 million grant by the James Tucker Foundation.

Example: (active voice) The James Tucker Foundation has given a $1 million grant to Midcity University.

Example: (active voice) The James Tucker Foundation is giving $1 million to Midcity University.

Write About It

Why is it important to try to use present-tense and active-voice verbs in your stories?

Use the following information to write a passive-voice sentence and then turn it into an active-voice sentence.

Winning bid: The Johnstone Construction Company

Passive-voice sentence:

Active-voice sentence:

NAMES

Most online news stories will include names. Be sure names are spelled correctly and be sure you've got the right person doing the right thing. In the heat of battle, it's easy to have the wrong person doing the wrong thing. Always double- or triple-check to be sure you haven't transposed names and activities. Always double- or triple-check the spelling of a name every time it appears in a story.

On the first reference to a person, use his or her full first and last name. When specific identification is needed, as in death, crime or award stories, it's a good idea to include middle initials, too. On subsequent references, use the person's last name only. Occasionally, in light, feature-type stories, you can use a person's first name on subsequent references. You also can use a child's first name rather than his or her last name on subsequent references.

Example: Sen. Richard S. Nelson is the newest member of the Midcity University Hall of Fame. Nelson will be inducted in a formal ceremony later this year.

Example: Gary Foster loves his job. Gary makes a living making other people laugh.

Example: Many experts say 16-year-old Kona Valenzuela is the next Tiger Woods. Kona has won every golf tournament he's entered for the past five years.

Full middle names are rarely used. Middle names are appropriate when a person has become well-known using the middle name. In addition, if including a middle name helps to distinguish the person from other people with the same first and last name, use it.

Example: Sarah Jessica Parker, Sarah Michelle Gellar, Ruth Bader Ginsberg, Billy Bob Thornton, Hillary Rodham Clinton, George Washington Carver

Example: James Allen Smith is the new Midcity Police Chief. He replaces James Edward Smith.

Nicknames should be used only when a person has become very well-known by his or her nickname. When a nickname is included with a person's given first and last name, place quotation marks around the nickname.

Example: Leonard "Ted" McFadden, Jake "The Snake" Taylor, Billy "The Kid" Jones, Lee "Hacksaw" Hamilton, Thomas "Hit Man" Hearns, Anne "The Sports Babe" Anderson

Write About It

List FIVE tips for using names in online news stories.

1.

2.

3.

4.

5.

TITLES

Quite often, you need to include a person's title with his or her name. Titles are good ways to distinguish one James Smith from all the other men named James Smith. Titles also can provide a great deal of information about a person in a nice, neat, concise package.

You should spell out completely and capitalize formal titles that are placed immediately before a person's name. Normally, titles are used only on the first reference to a person. On subsequent references, just the person's last name is used.

Example: Director of Communications Laurie Davies will serve on the committee. Davies will be joined by several students and staff members.

Some titles should be abbreviated when they precede a name.

Example: Dr., Gov., Lt. Gov., Rep., Sen., Mr., Mrs., Ms.

The title of Dr. should be reserved for a person who legally can prescribe medicine. If you choose to use the title of Dr. for a person who has earned a doctoral degree (Ph.D., Ed.D., etc.), be sure your readers will know the person is not a licensed doctor, dentist or psychiatrist.

Example: Dr. Jonathan Freedman is the new team physician.

Example: Dr. Janice Jacobs, a history professor at Midcity University, has written another book about slavery.

Affiliation with a political party can be designated by using the initials D or R to convey whether a member of Congress is a Democrat or Republican. The letter is capitalized and linked by a hyphen to the abbreviation for the state or city/town represented. The entire construction is set off from the person's name by commas.

Example: Sen. Margaret Cho, D-Calif., is expected to testify.

Example: Rep. Darin Kim, R-San Diego, did not attend the meeting.

You should lowercase and spell out titles that are used without a person's name.

Example: The quarterback said he wanted to see another doctor to get a second opinion.

You should lowercase titles that are placed after a name. Such titles should be separated from the name with commas.

Example: Fernando Castro, a professor at Midcity University, will be the speaker.

If you need to indicate someone is a "junior" or "senior," abbreviate Jr. and Sr. and place the designation immediately after the full first and last name of a person. **Do not** separate Jr. or Sr. with a comma. On subsequent references, if you need to distinguish son from father, use "elder" or "younger" before the last name of the person. You also can use roman numerals to indicate the continued use of a family name.

Example: Benjamin Valenzuela Jr. is the new CEO of 24-Hour Fitness.

Example: Benjamin Valenzuela III was drafted in the first round by the New York Yankees.

Example: The elder Valenzuela missed the younger Valenzuela's high school graduation ceremony.

Courtesy Titles

The courtesy titles of Mr., Mrs., Ms. should be used only in direct quotes or when needed to distinguish a husband from a wife or a brother from a sister who uses the same last name. Courtesy titles should NOT be used if there is no chance that readers will be confused about who is being referred to on subsequent references.

Example: "I don't think Mr. Jones or Mrs. Moreno will attend the debate tonight," Murphy said.

Example: James R. Smith, 52, and Linda S. Smith, 49, are the newest members of the Midcity Unified School District's Board of Education. Mr. Smith is a professor at Midcity University. Ms. Smith is a real estate agent.

Example: (wrong) Lisa Marie Naguchi, 41, and Terence V. Boyd, 38, are the newest members of the Midcity Unified School District's Board of Education. Mrs. Naguchi is a professor at Midcity University. Mr. Boyd is a real estate agent.

Example: (better) Lisa Marie Naguchi, 41, and Terence V. Boyd, 38, are the newest members of the Midcity Unified School District's Board of Education. Naguchi is a professor at Midcity University. Boyd is a real estate agent.

Military Titles

Capitalize and abbreviate a military title used before a person's name. Lowercase and spell out military titles that are used without names.

Example: (with names) Gen., Col., Maj., Capt., Lt., Sgt., Cpl., Pvt., Adm., Cmdr.

Example: (without names) general, colonel, major, captain, lieutenant, sergeant, corporal, private, admiral, commander

Example: Capt. Jane Everts was looking forward to meeting the general.

Write About It

List FIVE tips for using a person's title in online newswriting.

1.

2.

3.

4.

5.

AGES

You can include a person's age to help distinguish him or her from others with the same name. Including a person's age also can provide some insight into why something may have occurred and/or what the significance of the occurrence might be. Ages normally follow the last name of a person and are expressed as numerals. When the age follows the last name, it is separated from the name by commas.

Example: LaDonna Jeter, 25, finished last.

Example: LaDonna Jeter, who is 25 years old, finished last.

Ages can be reported in a variety of ways. When you want to use someone's or something's age as an adjective before a name or other noun, use hyphens to link the numeral and "years old."

Example: 25-year-old LaDonna Jeter finished last.

Example: The 25-year-old building will be demolished.

If you need to refer to someone's age in a generic, non-specific way, place an "s" after the last numeral. **Do not** use an apostrophe.

Example: The woman was reported to be in her 40s.

Example: (wrong) The woman was reported to be in her 40's.

A female can be referred to as a "girl" if she is less than 18 years old. A male can be referred to as a "boy" if he is less than 18 years old.

Example: A South Midcity boy, 16, is the skateboarding champion.

Example: A West Midcity girl, 14, will play in the golf tournament.

ADDRESSES

Addresses can be used to help identify a person. Addresses normally are included immediately after a person's name and are set off from the name by commas. When you include numbers with street names, capitalize and abbreviate the address designation. When you do not include numbers with street names, spell out the address designation.

Always spell out such address designations as Alley, Road, Terrace, Lane, Circle, etc.

Example: (with numbers) Ave., Blvd., St., Dr.

Example: (without numbers) Avenue, Boulevard, Street, Drive

Example: Eric Wulfemeyer, 3695 Summerfield Dr., won the race.

Example: Eric Wulfemeyer lives on Summerfield Drive.

Write About It

List FIVE tips for using ages and addresses in online newswriting.

1.

2.

3.

4.

5.

CONTRACTIONS

Use contractions often to make your copy sound more conversational and informal.

Example:

Use it's for it is or it has.
Use isn't for is not.
Use won't for will not.
Use aren't for are not.
Use weren't for were not.
Use can't for cannot.
Use hadn't for had not
Use they're for they are.
Use they'll for they will.
Use you're for you are.

ATTRIBUTION

An attribution lets readers know where information came from. Online news writers should include attribution for opinions and when there is reasonable doubt about the factual nature of allegations, assertions or pronouncements. Attribution is not required when facts are reported.

Example:

Two people died in the crash. (No need for attribution)
The fire burned 100 acres. (No need for attribution)
Jim Buckalew is a great professor. (Attribution needed)
The oil companies are gouging consumers. (Attribution needed)

Attribution can be included at the beginning of a sentence, in the middle of a sentence or at the end of a sentence.

Example: Mayor Moore says his budget plan will save the city at least $10 million.

Example: According to Mayor Moore, his budget plan will save the city at least $10 million.

Example: "My budget plan will save the city at least $10 million," said Mayor Moore.

Example: "My budget plan will save the city at least $10 million," said Mayor Moore, "but we'll have to make some drastic cuts."

Example: According to a report in the *New York Times*, some Wall Street insiders are facing federal racketeering charges.

Example: A two-day strike by Midcity police officers is scheduled to start Monday, according to a Midcity Police Association email sent to members yesterday.

QUOTES

Paraphrased Quotes

Generally, it's a good idea to paraphrase the exact words of speakers. You can make comments clearer and more concise. Be sure to keep the meaning, though. Don't distort what the speaker said and meant to convey.

Example: Quote from Mayor Moore—"The budget plan that I unveiled today is a detailed, well-documented account of how the city can save at least $10 million."

Example: (paraphrased) Mayor Moore says his budget plan can save the city at least $10 million.

Direct Quotes

Sometimes sources express something so well, so unusually, so outrageously or so lamely that you will want to be sure readers know that you're quoting the exact words of the source. In addition, direct quotes are useful when you're dealing with sensitive and controversial material. When you do quote a person or document exactly, use the exact words. Don't add or delete words. Put quotation marks around the exact words used and name the speaker, document or web site.

Example: "I'm the greatest poker player in the world," Eric Wulf said.

Example: Eric Wulf jumped up on a chair and yelled at the top of his lungs, "I'm the greatest poker player in the world!"

Example: "At least 25 percent of NFL players use steroids," according to a report on the www.NFLinsider.com web site.

Fragmentary Quotes

Keep your use of fragmentary quotes to a minimum. If you aren't going to quote an entire comment or passage, simply use a paraphrase.

Example: Mayor Moore says he's not going to give up on his plan, because it's "the only way to save the city from bankruptcy."

Example: (better) Mayor Moore says he's not going to give up on his plan, because it's the only way the city can avoid bankruptcy.

Example: Valenzuela says her department has many "deep and serious" problems.

Example: (better) Valenzuela says her department has several serious problems.

Write About It

List FIVE tips for using attribution and quotes in online newswriting.

1.

2.

3.

4.

5.

PROFANITY, FACTUAL ERRORS, SLANG AND POOR GRAMMAR

When sources make factual errors or use profanity, slang or poor grammar, it gives online news writers some problems. You don't want to foist factual errors, profanity, slang and grammatically incorrect copy on your readers, yet you don't want to give an inaccurate impression of your sources by cleaning up their mistakes and inappropriate language.

One solution is eliminating the mistakes and inappropriate language, but letting your readers know what you did. Another solution is using universally recognized substitutions for profane words. A final solution is pointing out mistakes and inappropriate language to readers. Of course, this technique isn't likely to please your sources very much. Use good judgment when confronted with the profane comments, use of slang, grammatically incorrect and outright factual errors made by sources. Try to get the important information to your readers without offending them. Try to get the important information to your readers without burning sources you hope to use again.

Example: In a profanity-laced tirade, McMahon blasted the officials after the game.

Example: In a tirade that was extremely grammatically incorrect, McMahon blasted the officials after the game.

Example: Using the language of the street, McMahon blasted the officials after the game.

Example: McMahon said the officials called pass interference 15 times against the Tigers, but the officials actually called pass interference 10 times against the Tigers.

Example: "Those officials don't know s**t about football," McMahon said.

Example: "Those f– – – – –g officials should be ashamed of themselves," McMahon said.

Example: "I could kill those $&*%#@¢ officials," McMahon said.

Example: "Those were the 'bleeping' worst officials I've ever seen," McMahon said.

Write About It

List FIVE ways that you could deal with a source's use of profanity, slang, poor grammar or inaccurate information.

1.

2.

3.

4.

5.

NUMBERS

Generally, single-digit numbers that stand alone are spelled out as words. Two-digit to six-digit numbers are written using Arabic numerals. Seven-digit and higher numbers can be written using numerals and the words "million," "billion," "trillion," etc.

Example: one, two, three, four, five, six, seven, eight, nine

Example: 10, 100, 1,000, 10,000, 100,000, 999,999

Example: 1 million, 9 million, 52 million, 17 billion, 29 trillion

Spell out numbers at the beginning of a sentence.

Example: Fifteen people died in the crash.

Example: One-hundred-fifteen people died in the crash.

Ordinal Numbers
Ordinal numbers follow the same rules as cardinal numbers. Spell out single-digit ordinals and use Arabic numerals and the appropriate letter combination for two-digit and larger ordinal numbers.

Example: First, second, third, fourth, fifth, sixth, seventh, eighth, ninth

Example: 10th, 21st, 32nd, 43rd, 101st, 252nd, 883rd, 974th

Roman Numerals
Use Roman numerals sparingly. They can be used for wars and to express a sequence of descendents or items in a series.

Example: World War II

Example: King Henry VII

Example: Super Bowl XXXVIII

Example: Title IX

Example: Benjamin Valenzuela III

The following letters are used to express Roman numerals:

    I = 1
    V = 5
    X = 10
    C = 100
    D = 500
    M = 1,000

All numbers are formed by stringing the appropriate letters together and either adding or subtracting. The value of a letter that follows a letter of equal or greater value is added. The value of a letter that precedes a letter of greater value is subtracted.

Example: III = 3, IV = 4, VII = 7, XIX = 19, MMVI = 2,006

Fractions

When you need to report a fraction, spell out amounts less than one. Place a hyphen between the words used to express the fraction.

Example: one-third, three-fifths, nine-sixteenths

For specific amounts greater than one, use numerals.

Example: 1 1/2, 2 3/4, 5 5/8, 9 9/10

Decimals

Sometimes, you might want to convert a fraction to a decimal for clarity.

Example: 1 1/2 = 1.5, 2 3/4 = 2.75, 5 5/8=5.625, 9 9/10 = 9.9

Money

Use the dollar sign, $, with numerals to express amounts of money.

Example: $1, $10, $100, $1,000

Example: $1.25, $6.33, $10.50

If you don't report a specific figure, spell out the word "dollar(s)."

Example: Dollars aren't worth what they once were.

Example: You can't buy anything for less than a dollar at the new store.

Specified amounts of money take a singular verb.

Example: The $250,000 was the winning bid.

For amounts of money in excess of $1 million, use the combination of numerals and the word "million," "billion," "trillion," etc.

Example: $3 million, $7 billion, $9 trillion

Example: $3.25 million, $7.5 billion, $9.33 trillion

For amounts of money less than $1, use a combination of the word "cents" (lowercase) and numerals.

Example: 2 cents, 16 cents, 99 cents

Write About It

List FIVE tips for using numbers in online newswriting.

1.

2.

3.

4.

5.

ABBREVIATIONS

Generally, you should keep your use of abbreviations to a minimum. If readers will easily recognize an abbreviation or acronym, then use it, but if you think there might be some confusion about the meaning of an abbreviation or acronym, spell out the word(s). Organizations and groups should be identified by their full names on the first reference in a story, but they can be identified by an abbreviation or acronym on subsequent references.

Example: The Citizens Against Rip-Offs group is at it again. CAR members are blocking traffic on Interstate 15.

If a group has become well-known by its abbreviated name or acronym, use it.

Example: FBI, CIA, AARP, YMCA, NASA, NATO, NCAA, NAACP, ACLU

Days of the week are capitalized and never abbreviated in news stories. The days of the week can be abbreviated in charts or other tabular material.

Example: Mon., Tue., Wed., Thu., Fri., Sat., Sun.

Months are always capitalized. When used with a specific date, some months are abbreviated. When standing alone or with just a year, spell out the month. If you use a month with just a year, do not separate the year with a comma. If you use a month, day and year, set off the year with commas.

Example: (when used with a specific date) Jan., Feb., Aug., Sept., Oct., Nov., Dec.

Note: March, April, May, June, and July are always spelled out in text.

Example: He is supposed to leave sometime in January.

Example: We had more snow in December 2006 than we had in all of 2005.

Example: Kegel said he hopes June 1, 2010, will be a very special day.

Example: Aug. 28 was the warmest day of the year.

Months can be abbreviated in charts or other tabular material.

Example: Jan., Feb., Mar., Apr., May, Jun., Jul., Aug., Sep., Oct., Nov., Dec.

The names of states should be capitalized and spelled out when they stand alone in text. The names of most states should be abbreviated when they follow the name of a city or town or are used to indicate political party affiliation. Commas are used between the city/town and state and after the state name.

The names of the states that are not part of the contiguous United States and states with five or fewer letters are always spelled out.

Example: Alaska, Hawaii, Idaho, Iowa, Maine, Ohio, Texas, Utah

Example: (when used with a city/town) Ala., Ariz., Ark., Calif., Colo., Conn., Del., Fla., Ga., Ill., Ind., Kan., Ky., La., Md., Mass., Mich., Minn., Miss., Mo., Mont., Neb., Nev., N.H., N.J., N.M., N.Y., N.C., N.D., Okla., Ore., Pa., R.I., S.C., S. D., Tenn., Vt., Va., Wash., W.Va., Wis., Wyo.

Example: Melissa Wulfemeyer was born in New Mexico.

Example: Melissa Wulfemeyer was born in Las Cruces, N.M.

Example: Melissa Wulfemeyer was born in Las Cruces, N.M., in 1976.

Example: Melissa Wulfemeyer, D-Calif., is the new committee chairwoman.

Example: Melissa Wulfemeyer grew up in Honolulu, Hawaii.

Example: Melissa Wulfemeyer has lived in Portland, Ore., and Lima, Ohio.

MEASUREMENTS AND AMOUNTS

Lowercase and spell out measurement words and words that convey amounts.

Example: inch, inches, foot, feet, yard, yards, mile, miles, acre, acres, cup, cups, ounce, ounces, pint, pints, quart, quarts, gallon, gallons, ton, tons, cubic feet, cubic yards, centimeter, centimeters, millimeter, millimeters, meter, meters, kilometer, kilometers, grams, milliliter, milliliters, liter, liters

Example: four inches, 10 feet, nine yards, 100 miles, one acre, 12 ounces, 25 gallons, 16 tons, 100 meters, two liters

There are a few exceptions to the measurement/amounts rules. When you want to indicate that you're referring to "square" feet, etc., *square* is abbreviated. In addition, when you're referring to millimeters in film or weapons, *millimeter* is abbreviated.

Example: sq. inches, sq. feet, sq. yards, sq. miles

Example: 16 mm film, 9 mm handgun

SYMBOLS

Few symbols are used in online newswriting. The $ is permissible, of course, but ¢ is not. Cents is correct. Percent is used instead of %. At is used instead of @. Pound is used instead of #. And is used instead of &.

Example: $5, 25 cents, 33 percent, Lewis and Clark

Note: Percent takes a singular verb when it's used alone or when it's followed by a singular noun that is the object of the preposition *of*. Percent takes a plural verb when it's followed by a plural noun that is the object of the preposition *of*.

Example: "An average of 70 percent is passing in this course," the professor said.

Example: Only about 70 percent of the class was seated on time.

Example: Only about 70 percent of the students were seated on time.

Occasionally, the & is used as part of an organization's/company's official name. The @ can be used in email addresses.

Example: Ben & Jerry's, the law firm of Kegel & McFadden

Example: Professor Tim Wulfemeyer's email address is twulf@mail.sdsu.edu

---

Write About It

List TEN tips for using abbreviations, measurements, amounts and symbols in online newswriting.

1.

2.

3.

4.

5.

6.

7.

8.

9.

10.

TIME OF DAY

Generally, the exact time that events occur or things are announced is not important to include in stories. If you decide that it is critical for readers to know the exact time of an event, development or announcement, use numerals and a colon to separate hours from minutes. Use *a.m.* to indicate time after midnight, but before noon, and use *p.m.* to indicate time after noon, but before midnight. If there are no minutes associated with the time, use two zeroes to indicate that. Use *noon* for 12:00 p.m. and *midnight* for 12:00 a.m.

Example: 5:00 a.m., 6:15 a.m., 7:30 p.m., 11:45 p.m.

Example: The game will start at noon.

Example: The festival will end at midnight.

TIME ELEMENTS

Most of the time, online news writers should use such terms as "this morning," "this afternoon," "this evening" and "tonight." If your web site isn't being updated very often, it is better to use the days of the week rather than today, tonight, this morning, etc.

You should place the time element in a sentence where it seems most natural. The time element should be part of the flow of the sentence. It should not interrupt the flow. Generally, a time element can be placed at the beginning of a sentence, at the end of a sentence or right before or right after the verb.

Example: Two people died in a freak accident this morning.

Example: The meeting is scheduled to start at 7:30 tonight.

Example: Two people died in a freak accident Wednesday morning.

Example: On Wednesday morning, two people died in a freak accident.

Example: Two people died Wednesday morning in a freak accident.

Example: Five local firefighters were injured in an explosion this afternoon.

Example: This afternoon, five local firefighters were injured in an explosion.

Example: Five local firefighters this afternoon were injured in an explosion.

Example: Five local firefighters were injured this afternoon in an explosion.

Write About It

List FIVE tips for reporting time of day and using time elements in online newswriting.

1.

2.

3.

4.

5.

PUNCTUATION

Use punctuation marks to make your copy clearer and more understandable. Generally, you should follow the standard rules of punctuation. Occasionally, you might want to break a rule or two for effect, but keep such instances to a minimum. Some common usage of punctuation is included below.

Apostrophe—use to indicate possession, to substitute for missing letters or numbers and to indicate plurals of single letters. An apostrophe also is used to indicate a quote within a direct quote.

Example: Jackson's hat, the team's equipment, the billionaire's private jet

Example: it's (it is or it has), we've (we have)

Example: He's living in the 50's. (1950s)

Example: He earned four A's, two B's and two C's this year.

Example: "I thought I heard the woman say 'I never heard a thing' when she was questioned by the police," Stackhouse said.

Colon—use at the end of a sentence that introduces a list of things.

Example: Murdock mentioned three problems: the cost, lack of oversight and poor quality.

Comma—use to separate items in a series, to set off clauses and phrases, and to separate words of attribution from direct quotes. Commas also are used to separate ages, addresses and political party affiliation in text. Commas are placed after the names of cities and states when the city and state are listed consecutively.

Example: Emergency packs should include water, crackers, batteries and a flashlight.

Note: Normally, a comma is not placed before the conjunction "and."

Example: Anderson, the leading candidate during the early part of the campaign, is now five percentage points behind Munoz and Chang.

Example: Anderson said, "I ran a good race, but the voters preferred someone else."

Example: Sylvia Davis, 57, 1895 Emerald Heights Dr., suffered minor injuries in the crash.

Example: Sen. Clifford Albert, D-Calif., will be the keynote speaker.

Example: San Diego, Calif., will host Super Bowl XLVIII.

Dash—use to set off a list of things that is included within a phrase.

Example: Most employers focus on three things—honesty, punctuality, intelligence—when they make hiring decisions.

Ellipsis—use three periods (. . .) to indicate the deletion of one or more words from a quote, document or other source.

Example: (original quote) "I am not going to attend tonight's event, and I have let the sponsors of the event know that I will not be attending, because I cannot condone the abuse of animals at medical schools," Yamashita said.

Example: (rewritten quote) "I am not going to attend tonight's event . . . because I cannot condone the abuse of animals at medical schools."

Exclamation point—use to indicate strong emotion, surprise or disbelief.

Example: "Chargers rule!" shouted the fan as the players began to board the bus.

Hyphen—use to link words that form compound adjectives.

Example: The well-respected professor has decided to become a part-time instructor at a local trade school.

Period—use to indicate the end of declarative sentences. Use also after most letters that serve as abbreviations and acronyms.

Example: Four people died in the crash.

Example: Martin T. Boyd, U.S., Dr., Gov., Sen., Sgt., Lt., B.A., Ph.D.

Note: Some organizations have become well-known by their abbreviated names and, in many cases, the abbreviations **Do not** have periods after the letters.

Example: CIA, FBI, NOW, AARP, ABC, CBS, NBC, NASA, NAFTA

Question mark—use at the end of direct questions.

Example: Which candidates will participate in the debate?

Example: Who started the fight?

Note: A question mark is not used after an indirect question.

Example: Warburton wondered which candidates were going to participate in the debate.

Example: Larson wanted to know who started the fight.

Quotations marks—use to indicate the beginning and ending of the exact words of a full or partial direct quotation. Use also around the titles of books, movies, plays, songs, TV programs, etc. Use also to identify nicknames and to indicate ironic elements associated with a word or words.

Example: "I can't believe I survived," Owens said.

Example: Owens says the experience was "life-changing."

Example: "American Idol" is the top-rated television program in America.

Example: Theodore "Ted" McFadden is the new men's golf coach at Midcity University.

Example: The "peace rally" turned ugly when a shoving match broke out.

Note: Generally speaking, periods and commas are placed within quotation marks. Dashes, semicolons, question marks and exclamation points are placed within quotation marks when they apply to the quoted material, but they go outside quotation marks when they apply to the entire sentence.

Example: "I will not run for re-election," Lewis said.

Example: Lewis said, "I will not run for re-election."

Example: "What a great concert!" the young girl exclaimed.

Example: Who was the main star in "Animal House"?

Semicolon—use to separate items in a series when the items are lengthy and/or items include segments that include commas.

Example: The categories are as follows: dogs and cats; hamsters, gerbils, guinea pigs, mice and rats; horses, cows, sheep and pigs; birds, fish and snakes.

Write About It

List TEN tips for using punctuation marks correctly in online newswriting.

1.

2.

3.

4.

5.

6.

7.

8.

9.

10.

BUILDING A STORY

Inverted Pyramid Model

A news story, like any good story, has a beginning, middle and end. In journalism, the beginning of a story generally is referred to as the "lead." The middle of the story often is referred to as the "body." The end of the story often is referred to as the "conclusion."

One of the traditional models used for organizing a news story is the "inverted pyramid." You begin the story with the most important and/or interesting information and proceed, including the second most important information second, the third most important information third and so on until you run out of time, space or information.

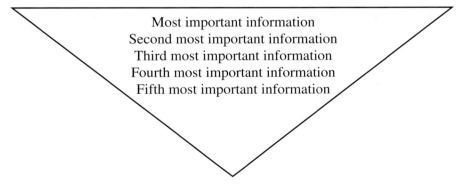

Most important information
Second most important information
Third most important information
Fourth most important information
Fifth most important information

Main Points and Supporting Evidence Model

You can also organize your story by using a series of main points and the supporting evidence associated with each of the main points. After you've gathered all the information you're going to need to write your story, identify the main points and then link important supporting evidence to each main point.

Prioritize the main points and begin your story by leading with the top-rated main point. Include an appropriate amount of supporting evidence—enough to convince readers that the main point is important—and then move on to main point number two. You continue including main points and the associated supporting evidence until you've reached your assigned number of words or run out of significant information.

This technique is much like traditional "outlining" as a preparation for writing a term paper. You can even use the mechanics of "outlining." Many professionals use Arabic numbers and letters. Some use symbols. Use whatever works best for you.

Example:
I. Cost of gasoline going up.
   A. New average price is $2.95 per gallon for regular unleaded this week. Previous week's average price was $2.89.
   B. Main reason for increase————several refineries closed for repairs so production reduced.
II. Consumer groups suggesting protests and boycotting major companies.
   A. People advised to buy gasoline from independents.
   B. People urged to write protest letters or emails to major companies and Congressional representatives.

Example:
1. Cost of gasoline going up.
   1a. New average price is $2.95 per gallon for regular unleaded this week. Previous week's average price was $2.89.
   1b. Main reason for increase—several refineries closed for repairs so production reduced.
2. Consumer groups suggesting protests and boycotting major companies.
   2a. People advised to buy gasoline from independents.
   2b. People urged to write protest letters or emails to major companies and Congressional representatives.

Example:
*****Cost of gasoline going up.
   *****A. New average price is $2.95 per gallon for regular unleaded this week. Previous week's average price was $2.89.
   *****B. Main reason for increase—several refineries closed for repairs so production reduced.
  ****Consumer groups suggesting protests and boycotting major companies.
   ****A. People advised to buy gasoline from independents.
   ****B. People urged to write protest letters or emails to major companies and Congressional representatives.

Write About It

Which story-organization model do you prefer? Why?

Leads
Summary Lead

The summary lead summarizes much of the critical information that you want to share with your readers. It will often contain most, if not all, of the 5Ws and the H—Who, What, Where, When, Why and How. While the summary lead can be effective in certain instances, generally, it's not a good idea to try to cram so much information into the first couple of sentences of an online news story. You certainly want to include the who, what, where, when, why and how in most stories, but you'll normally space them out over the entire story.

Example:

A West Midcity woman, Melissa L. Wulfe, 22, was named Midcity University's "Woman of the Year" last night at MU's Hunter Arena. A committee of faculty members, administrators and student leaders picked Wulfe, who has a 4.0 grade point average and is active in several university and community charitable organizations.

> Who = A West Midcity woman, Melissa L. Wulfe
> What = Named Midcity University's "Woman of the Year"
> Where = MU's Hunter Arena
> When = Last night
> Why = Wulfe has a 4.0 GPA and is active in a variety of charitable organizations
> How = Selected by a committee

Single-Element Lead

The single-element lead is the most common lead used in newswriting. It emphasizes the single, most-important, most-significant piece of information you have to share with your readers. Whatever you decide is the most critical fact to present is featured in the lead. Quite often it is the "what" of the story, but a combination of the "what" and the "how" is fairly common, too. In fact, it is not unusual to incorporate several of the 5Ws and the H in a single-element lead. You just keep the focus on a single issue, fact or development.

Example: A major brush fire is burning out of control in West Midcity.

Example: Sen. Hillary Clinton is the new President of the United States.

Example: The San Diego Padres are the world champions of baseball.

Example: A large tornado is racing toward Midcity.

Multiple-Element Lead

The multiple-element lead is good for stories that cover a variety of related, but different decisions, issues, events and developments. Such leads are often called "umbrella" or "blanket" leads, because they cover more than one specific person, place or thing. Such leads are good for stories about a series of votes by the Senate, House of Representatives, Board of Supervisors or City Council. They're good for stories that deal with a number of traffic accidents, police actions or fires that occur on the same day or over a selected period of time—holiday weekends, vacation periods, etc.

Blanket or umbrella leads are good for stories that deal with multiple decisions by the U.S. Supreme Court. They're good for stories that deal with corporate changes and other business-related developments.

Example: The Board of Supervisors approved spending for five major projects this morning.

Example: Six people died in three separate traffic accidents overnight in Midcity.

Example: Three brush fires are burning in Midcity this morning.

Example: The U.S. Supreme Court has ruled on four major cases.

Delayed-Identification Lead

Most of the time, you'll want to include the "who" of a story in the lead. Quite often, though, you might want to delay the name until the second paragraph or even later. You might want to increase suspense or you might decide that what the person did is more important than his or her name. Maybe including the person's title or what he or she does for a living will be more informative than using the name.

Example:
A West Midcity woman is the new "Woman of the Year" at Midcity University. She was selected from 15 candidates last night at the annual awards banquet. She has a 4.0 GPA and is active with a variety of charitable organizations.

Melissa L. Wulfe, 22, is the first local woman to be selected in more than 10 years. She is majoring in journalism and hopes to work as an online journalist when she receives her degree in May.

Question Lead

Occasionally, it's appropriate to begin a story with a question. The question lead should be used sparingly, though. People become news consumers because they want answers to questions. They can become annoyed when they're confronted with more questions as part of a news story. Besides, if you ask a question in the lead and the answer is "no," you've likely lost your readers. It might be better to recast the lead to encourage readers to read on rather than give them a reason to stop reading.

In addition, many advertisements begin with questions and many people have developed a sense that whenever they hear or see a question in the media, it means some sort of advertisement is on the way. This can cause readers to mentally or even physically tune out whatever follows the opening question. Don't completely eliminate the question lead from your arsenal, though. In certain situations, it can be an effective way to draw readers into your story.

Example: Have you ever dreamed of owning and programming your own radio station?

Example: (recast) If you've ever dreamed of owning and programming your own radio stations, podcasting is for you.

Example: Do you want to get ahead in life?

Example: (recast) If you want to get ahead in life, get organized.

Quotation Lead

When someone has said something that is so beautifully expressed or so lamely put that you feel compelled to share it with readers, consider using a quotation to begin your story. Just like the question lead, the quotation lead should be used sparingly. Be selective. Save the technique for the extraordinary quote.

Example:

"This is the greatest honor of my life."
That's what Melissa L. Wulfe, 22, said when she was named "Woman of the Year" at Midcity University last night.

Example:

"I will not run for re-election."
Mayor Ronald Moore shocked a packed house at the Board of Supervisors' meeting last night with that announcement.

Shocker Lead

A shocker lead can be used when you're dealing with outrageous information or when you just want to spice up rather routine information. A shocker lead can be a regular sentence, but it's often a phrase or even just one word. The idea is to "shock" readers into wanting to find out more about the issue, event or development. Be careful and selective with your use of the "shocker lead." Use it too often and it loses its shock value. You remember the story about the little boy who cried "wolf," right?

Example:

Death.
It comes for all of us.

Example:

The major oil companies are "stealing" money from consumers.
At least that's the claim of Citizens Against Rip-Offs.

Example:

Weirdo. Freak. Nerd. Doofus.
And these are the "good" terms that have been used to describe Mark Nix.

Direct Address Lead

The direct address lead can be an effective way to engage readers. In the direct address lead, you speak directly to the individual reader. It's designed to get readers immediately thinking about the issues, events or developments featured in your story. It forces readers to interact with you from the beginning of the story. Of course, the risk is that readers might not see themselves as part of the group that should be interested in the information you have to share. If that happens, they leave you immediately rather than stay with you.

Example: If you're driving around with an expired license, you're driving on borrowed time.

Example: You need a formal will or your loved ones might not be able to enjoy your legacy.

Example: Do you always know where your children are after 10:00 p.m. every night?

Example: You should have a retirement plan.

Example: Are you tired of being ripped off?

Compare-Contrast Lead

The compare-contrast lead is a good way to get readers thinking about alternatives to the status quo or traditional solutions to problems. In addition, it's a good way to begin stories that deal with issues that have multiple dimensions. It's also good for stories that deal with issues that have relatively equally strong pro and con dimensions.

Example: San Diego's beaches and bays get polluted every time it rains, but a Midcity University professor thinks he has a plan that can change that.

Example: Most experts agree that the over-crowding at Midcity University will take some time to correct, but two local businesswomen say they can speed up the process and save the university millions of dollars while doing it.

Example: Mayor Ronald Moore's budget plan includes some deep programmatic and personnel cuts, but it also calls for increasing staffing in several city departments.

Example: San Diego's new city manager has his supporters, but he has a large number of detractors, too.

Verbless Lead

The verbless lead, as the name implies, does not include a verb. Online news writers should not overuse verbless leads, but such leads can be effective when used occasionally. Instead of including a "there is" or a "there was" at the beginning of a sentence, just start with whatever follows the "there is" or "there was."

Example: (wrong) There were eight traffic-related deaths over the holiday weekend.

Example: (better) Eight traffic-related deaths over the holiday weekend.

Example: (wrong) There is some big news coming out of city hall this morning.

Example: (better) Big news coming out of city hall this morning.

Example: (wrong) There is a big brush fire burning in West Midcity.

Example: (better) A big brush fire in West Midcity.

Narrative Lead

The narrative lead is much like true storytelling. The narrative lead begins with the first thing that happened and then the rest of the story proceeds in chronological order through all of the other things that happened. No effort is made to select the most interesting or most significant aspect and lead with it. The narrative lead is not used very often in online newswriting and is reserved for the occasional feature story or in-depth look at an event, issue or development.

Example: Yesterday morning started out like most mornings for Sharon Ishida. She woke up at 6:00 a.m., fixed herself breakfast, showered and dressed for work. But when she opened the front door, the routine became the unbelievable.

Vague/Teaser Lead

The vague/teaser lead is used by some writers who hope that if readers are provided incomplete information or information that is unclear, they will want to read more. It's a big gamble and one that is rarely justified. Being obscure or leaving out important details on purpose is no way to treat readers. Of course, a headline will help add some useful information, but why chance losing readers with a vague, confusing lead?

Example: It's an idea that has been tried before, but has never worked. It sounds promising, but it's expensive and demands a complete reorganization of the city's administrative structure.

Example: (better) The idea of charging fees for the use of public parks has been tried before and it's never worked.

Example: Most users are disgusted. People who see it being used have been known to lose their lunch. Even the inventor thinks it should be taken off the market.

Example: (better) The inventor of the world's first dog-poop-hardening napkins is having second thoughts about his invention.

Write About It

Which types of leads do you think should be used most often in online newswriting? Why?

Body Building

The body of the story normally flows relatively easily after you've written the lead. The body should be built on the "promises" made in the lead. Give information to support the facts and allegations made in the lead. Flesh out the details. Explain what's significant and why. Explain why people should care about the events, issues and developments. Be sure to include the "meaning" of the events, issues and developments. Be sure to answer the question, "So what?"

As covered earlier, the body can be built using a series of main points and the accompanying supporting evidence. Be sure to provide supporting evidence for each main point, though. Your story should not simply be a series of main points. You need to provide supporting evidence to convince readers that the main points are significant.

Example:
The cost of gasoline is going up. Again. The new average price is $2.95 per gallon for regular unleaded. Last week, the average price was $2.89.

The main reason for the increase, according to experts, is the closing of several refineries for regularly scheduled maintenance. Since demand for gasoline continues to be strong and production has been reduced, prices had to go up.

A local consumer group is suggesting that people let the major oil companies and government leaders know how upset they are. A spokesman for Citizens Against Rip-Offs, Zachary Moore, says CAR wants people to boycott the major oil companies and buy their gasoline from independents. In addition, CAR is urging people to send protest letters and emails to their Congressional representatives.

Endings
Good online news stories feature strong endings. Your conclusion can take one of four basic forms:

1. Background Information

2. Back to the Future

3. Links to the Lead

4. Final Piece of Supporting Evidence

You can end with some background information. Include some past achievements of the major players in your story and/or provide a bit of an historical perspective.

Example: Wulfemeyer is the author or co-author of six textbooks, 40 refereed journal articles and 50 research papers. He's been teaching at San Diego State University for 25 years.

You can end with information about the future. Include what likely will happen next. Where does the bill go next? What's the next likely step in the process? When will the final vote be taken? When's the next meeting scheduled?

Example: The bill now goes to the Senate.

Example: The Board of Supervisors will vote on the matter next week.

Example: Gov. Sorenson is expected to veto the bill.

You can end your story with information that links directly back to what was covered in the lead. You can use the same references and/or complete the circle back to the lead by explaining how the person, place or thing is dealing with or has dealt with the events, issues or developments highlighted in the lead. Be careful to avoid platitudes and awkward constructions in your attempts to link your ending with your lead. If you don't see a natural, obvious link, don't force it. Use a different ending.

Example:

(lead) Mayor Ronald Moore is hoping to drum up support for his budget proposal at a series of town-hall meetings this month.

(ending) It's clear Moore will have to beat the drum long and hard if he expects to get the public support he needs so badly.

You can end your story with the last piece of supporting evidence you have for your last main point. Frankly, this is probably the most common ending for most stories. Try to use some of the other ending methods, though, whenever you can. They're stronger and leave readers with a greater sense of finality and contentment that they have acquired the facts and opinions they need to help them feel informed and to help them make the important decisions in their lives.

Example: Moore hopes his month-long push to whip up public support for his budget plan will convince the Board of Supervisors to vote his way.

Example: The exhibits will be open until 11:00 p.m.

Write About It

What type of ending do you feel most comfortable using most often? Why?

SECTION TWO
Pictures, Graphics, Audio and Video

Incorporating pictures, graphics, audio and video with text makes news web sites much more interesting, inviting, engaging and interactive for readers. Online news writers need to know how to write to pictures and graphics and how to set up and write for audio/video cuts. Quality web sites weave pictures, graphics, audio and video into the fabric of their content rather than layer such elements on top of traditional text. In other words, quality web sites strive to create segments that look very much like online versions of newspapers, magazines, radio newscasts and television newscasts.

WRITING FOR PICTURES

Writing text that is connected to a picture requires online news writers to provide concise information that helps readers make sense of the picture. Most of the time, picture captions or cutlines are limited to a single sentence. Don't try to cram too much information into the captions or cutlines and don't simply describe what readers can see for themselves. Captions or cutlines should supplement what readers can see when they look at a picture.

If you're asked to write a caption or cutline for a picture, examine the picture carefully or read a description of the picture carefully. Identify the elements of the picture that you think readers will notice right away. You likely will not have to provide information about the obvious aspects in the picture. Instead, decide what supplemental information needs to be provided to help readers gain a greater understanding of the significance of what they can see for themselves.

Picture: Shows a 2005 Ford Mustang and a 2004 Dodge Durango damaged after a collision at the corner of Market Street and First Avenue this morning.

Example: (wrong) A 2005 Ford Mustang and a 2004 Dodge Durango collided at the corner of Market Street and First Avenue this morning.

Example: (better) A malfunctioning traffic light is blamed for this collision at the corner of Market Street and First Avenue this morning.

Picture: Shows fire department helicopter dropping water on brush fire in West Midcity. Flames and smoke visible.

Example: (wrong) Fire department helicopter drops water on brush fire in West Midcity.

Example: (better) A brush fire in West Midcity burned 300 acres, but was contained by 3:00 p.m. Wednesday.

WRITING FOR MAPS AND CHARTS

Writing a caption or cutline for a map or a chart requires the same procedure as writing a caption or cutline for a picture. Examine the map or chart or a description of the map or chart. Determine what readers can ascertain on their own. Think about what information needs to be presented to enhance reader understanding of the map or chart.

Map: Shows several California cities, including Los Angeles, Anaheim, Palm Springs and San Diego. A large, red X is located near Palm Springs.

Example: (wrong) The earthquake's center was near Palm Springs and was felt in Los Angeles, Anaheim, Palm Springs and San Diego.

Example: (better) A 5.2 earthquake hit near Palm Springs Tuesday afternoon and was felt in nearby cities, but no deaths, injuries or significant property damage reported.

Chart: Shows three bars. One represents the national average on the latest round of SAT scores. It is topped with the number 1585. The second represents the state average on the latest round of SAT scores. It is topped with the number 1605. The third represents the Midcity average on the latest round of SAT scores. It is topped with the number 1595.

Example: (wrong) Midcity students averaged 1,595 on this year's SAT. The national average was 1,585. The state average was 1,605.

Example: (better) Midcity students beat the national average on this year's SAT, but despite more preparation courses and tutoring sessions, local students still scored below the state average.

SETTING UP AUDIO AND VIDEO CUTS FROM NEWSMAKERS

Introductions for audio and video cuts from newsmakers should attract reader attention and prepare them for the content of the cut. Use complete sentences to introduce audio/video cuts and be sure to name the speaker.

Example: Mayor Moore says his re-development plan has three major advantages.

Click Here to Hear Mayor Moore

Do not use the "when asked if, here's what he had to say" method to introduce an audio/video cut. It's awkward, unnatural and the lazy writer's way of doing things.

Example: (wrong) When asked if his plan would work, here's what Mayor Moore said.

Click Here to Hear Mayor Moore

Be sure you avoid the "echo effect" of writing an introduction that is basically repeated by the speaker. Use different words in your introduction, but be sure to set up the cut well. The cut should flow naturally from the introduction, much like a conversation or chat would flow.

Example: (wrong) Mayor Moore says his plan cannot fail.

Click Here to Hear Mayor Moore

Audio plays: "My plan cannot fail. It's fool-proof and cost-effective."

Example: (better) Mayor Moore says his plan will be successful.

   Click Here to Hear Mayor Moore

Audio plays: "My plan cannot fail. It's fool-proof and cost-effective."

Online news writers must make note of the content of audio/video cuts from newsmakers and be sure to set up the cuts effectively, completely and compellingly. It is critical that online news writers provide adequate information prior to an audio/video cut to help readers make sense out of the content of the cut. For example, if a newsmaker mentions a number, refers to something specific or mentions a name in the cut, be sure enough information has been provided prior to the cut so readers will understand what the newsmaker is talking about.

Example:
Mayor Moore says the key to his plan is the 10 percent increase in the Hotel Occupancy Tax and he's hoping Supervisor Stan Davis won't fight him this time around.

   Click Here to Hear Mayor Moore

Audio plays: "If the guy gets on board with the proposed H-O-T increase, he'll be doing the city a big service."

If the supervisor's name had not been mentioned prior to the cut and if the Hotel Occupancy Tax had not been mentioned and if the level of the proposed increase in the tax had not been mentioned, readers would not be able to make much sense out of the cut, would they?

SETTING UP AUDIO AND VIDEO PACKAGES FROM REPORTERS

Occasionally, audio and/or video versions of complete stories or "packages" from reporters are made available online. Whenever possible, incorporate an aspect of what the story is about, where the reporter had to go or what the reporter had to do to gather the information for the story.

Example: Reporter Mollie Cooney was front and center for all the protesting.

   Click Here for Cooney Report

Example: Reporter Mollie Cooney risked life and limb to find out what was going on.

   Click Here for Cooney Report

Example: Reporter Mollie Cooney has both sides of this controversial issue.

   Click Here for Cooney Report

Don't stretch too far to incorporate out-of-the-ordinary aspects into your reporter introductions. If you can't come up with meaningful, natural introductions that include what the reporter did or where he or she went, simply use one of the standard introduction lines.

Example: Mollie Cooney has a full report.

Click Here for Cooney Report

Example: Reporter Mollie Cooney has more.

Click Here for Cooney Report

Example: Reporter Mollie Cooney has the details.

Click Here for Cooney Report

WRITING FOR VIDEO

It is not uncommon for online news writers to write scripts for video that will be streamed on web sites. The key to effective writing to video is having the words and pictures complement each other. What readers see is what they should hear about. It is not always easy to create consistent audio-video matching, but that should be your goal.

Writing to video can be done in three basic ways.

1. A script can be written and the video edited to match the words.

2. Video can be edited and the script written to match the scenes in the video.

3. Video editors and writers can work together to ensure maximum matching.

The most difficult method for writers, of course, is to be presented with a pre-edited piece of video and be asked to write copy to match the video scenes. The other two methods of writing to video normally do not create as many problems for writers.

If you're asked to write copy for a piece of pre-edited video, watch the video to get a sense of what is depicted. If you're not presented with a list of the video scenes and their lengths, create one for yourself. If you can't watch the video, study a list of the video scenes carefully.

Look for what are called "matching points." Matching points are major people, places or things; shifts in topic or subject; and shifts in geographic locations. The first time major people, places or things appear in video, they should be identified while they're being seen. Every significant change in topic of subject should be mentioned when it occurs. Every significant change in geographic locations should be mentioned when it occurs. "Filler" scenes that are placed between the major people, places, things, topics, subjects and locations can be used to move gracefully between the major matching points.

News videos comprise three basic types of scenes.

1. Cover shots—wide-angle views of locations or activities

2. Medium shots—usually two to three people or things

3. Close-up shots—tight shots of faces, hands or one person or thing

Scenes called cutaways or cut-ins are normally medium shots that are used to transition from scenes of main action or main participants. Such scenes normally do not contain major people, places or things, so writers can use such scenes to help the logical flow from one main action/person/place to another.

Once you've examined the provided or created "shot list" of the scenes and their lengths, you should create a concise outline of how your story will run. You use the outline to help you hit all of the matching points.

Example:

   Shot List:

1.	Cover shot of dog show	:06
2.	Medium shot of celebrity judge	:04
3.	Cover shot of audience	:06
4.	Close-up shot of terrier	:04
5.	Medium shot of schipperke	:04
6.	Cover shot of dog show	:06

   Outline:

1. Basic information about dog show
2. Celebrity judge
3. Size of audience
4. Winning dog
5. Second place dog
6. More basic information

Now you have a road map to follow to create your story. The next thing you have to be concerned with is the length of each scene. In the above example, you or the person reading your script will need to be talking about the celebrity judge six seconds after the video begins. The winning dog will have to be mentioned 16 seconds after the video begins. The second-place dog will have to be mentioned at the 20-second mark.

If you use 60-character lines, one line equals about three seconds. If you're counting words, about three words equals one second. You'll have to experiment a bit, though, to determine how best to make the matching work well.

Example: The dog show is the first of its kind in Midcity. Proceeds
from the event will go to help our city's homeless children.
One of the judges was local TV personality James Rada of
K-T-I-M's "Cartoonville."
More than three thousand people packed the McKenzie
Ballroom at the Midcity Grand Hotel for the three-hour show.
The big winner was "Tango," a Jack Russell terrier. He was
named best in his division and best in show.
The runner up was "Kai," a Schipperke. He also won the best-
trained dog award.
Organizers say they're so happy with how things worked out
this year that they're already making plans for next year's show.

You can use pauses to help improve matching. Pauses can be effective, especially if natural sound is available as part of your video. You can indicate pauses by using periods and the word "pause."

Example: ....

Example: ....Pause....................

Take a look at how the dog show story script would look with a few pauses.

Example: The dog show is the first of its kind in Midcity. Proceeds
from the event will go to help our city's homeless children.
One of the judges was local TV personality James Rada.

....

More than three-thousand people attended the show
.....................Pause...........................
The big winner was "Tango," a Jack Russell terrier.

....

The runner up was "Kai," a Schipperke.

....

Organizers say they're so happy with how things worked out
this year that they're already making plans for next year's show.

Example:

Information:

1. Fire at a house, 4581 North Pine Glen Way.
2. House and six-car garage damaged.
3. Both house and garage fully engulfed when firefighters arrived.
4. Fire started at 5:00 a.m. Tuesday.
5. Firefighters fought blaze for about two hours.
6. Firefighters spent about one hour cleaning up and checking for hot spots.
7. Midcity Fire Department Captain Caitlyn S. McFadden reports that fire started in the garage when a gas water heater overheated and ignited some newspapers that were being saved for a recycling fund drive.
8. McFadden estimate for damage to the house and garage: $1.5 million.

Shot List:

1. Cover shot of burning house   :06
2. Medium shot of firefighters with hose :04
3. Close-up of Caitlyn McFadden   :04
4. Medium shot of charred water heater   :06
5. Cover shot of mopping up activities   :05

Outline:

1. Basic information about the fire
2. Firefighters
3. McFadden quote about damage and cause of fire
4. Details about water heater malfunction
5. Basic information about mopping up

Video Script:

The fire started at about 5:00 Tuesday morning. The house and the detached six car garage were fully engulfed when firefighters arrived on the scene. They battled the blaze for a little more than two hours.
Fire Captain Caitlyn McFadden estimated the damage at about $1.5 million.
She says the fire started when the gas water heater in the garage overheated and ignited some old newspapers.
Firefighters spent about an hour cleaning up and being sure that all the hot spots were taken care of.

Write About It

List TEN tips for writing for pictures, graphics, audio and video.

1.

2.

3.

4.

5.

6.

7.

8.

9.

10.

Making Good Online Newswriting Better

The English language has a number of idiosyncratic aspects that cause problems for even the best writers. Many words sound the same, but are spelled differently and have different meanings. How a word is used in a sentence can often dictate what form it should take. In this section, we'll cover a variety of general tips for improving good online newswriting.

In most cases, the problematic words and phrases are "red flags" that should cause you to stop and think about usage, spelling, form and meaning. All writers have bad days. All writers can get distracted. All writers can be up against deadlines. All writers make mistakes. The important thing is to recognize the "red flag" words and phrases and always take a few extra seconds to analyze the situation to determine which word is correct.

CORRECT USAGE

A vs. An

The article *a* is used before a word that begins with a consonant or a word that sounds as if it begins with a consonant. The article *an* is used before a word that begins with a vowel or a word that sounds as if it begins with a vowel.

Example: a bike, a shop, a person, a united front

Example: an apple, an elephant, an umbrella, an hour

Accept vs. Except

Accept means to take, to receive, and to agree to something. *Except* means to exclude or other than.

Example: The man said it was an honor to accept the award on behalf of his brother.

Example: Every candidate attended except Sen. Adonis Marin.

Advice vs. Advise

Advice is a noun that means counsel, suggestions or recommendations. *Advise* is a verb that means to give counsel, suggestions or recommendations.

Example: The police officer offered some good advice about how to deal with bullies.

Example: The police officer planned to advise students about how to deal with bullies.

Affect vs. Effect

When *affect* is used as a verb, it means to influence. When *affect* is used as a noun, it refers to such psychological aspects as emotions, feelings or moods. When *effect* is used as a noun, it means a result. When *effect* is used a verb, it means to cause or bring about.

It is relatively rare to use *affect* as a noun and it is equally rare to use *effect* as a verb, so a good, general decision rule to follow is when you need a verb, use *affect* and when you need a noun, use *effect*.

Example: Concerns about money can affect any decision-making process.

Example: Concerns about money had a negative effect on the decision-making process.

Example: (rare) The affect of estrangement contributed to his odd behavior.

Example: (rare) The governor said we need to effect a change in the zoning.

Aid vs. Aide vs. AIDS

Aid means assistance. An *aide* is an assistant. *AIDS* is a disease (Acquired Immune Deficiency Syndrome).

Example: Providing aid to someone who needs it is gratifying experience.

Example: The senator's aide may be called to testify.

Example: The company has decided to give $10 million to support AIDS research.

Allusion vs. Illusion

An *allusion* is an indirect reference to something or a casual mention of something. An *illusion* is something unreal or a false impression.

Example: The allusion he made about the war being similar to a football game seemed inappropriate.

Example: The idea that the economy is starting to improve is an illusion.

Alumnus vs. Alumna

People who graduate from a school, college or university are alums. An *alumnus* is a male graduate. *Alumni* is used to refer to more than one male graduate. *Alumni* also is used to refer to a group of male and female graduates. An *alumna* is a female graduate. *Alumnae* is used to refer to more than one female graduate.

Example: Ronald R. Moore is an alumnus of Midcity University.

Example: Susan L. Moore is an alumna of Midcity University.

Example: Stan Davis and Tim Wulfemeyer are alumni of Santana High School.

Example: Melissa Wulfemeyer and Sarah Schultz are alumnae of Monte Vista High School.

Example: Donna Miller and Tim Wulfemeyer are alumni of Santana High School.

Among vs. Between

Among is used when three or more people, places or things are involved. *Between* is used when just two people, places or things are involved.

Example: The proceeds from the estate were divided equally among the five surviving children.

Example: The trouble between the two cousins started more than 20 years ago.

Blond vs. Blonde

Use *blond* when referring to a male with yellowish/golden hair. Use *blond* as an adjective when referring to something that is light-colored. Use *blonde* when referring to a female with yellowish/golden hair.

Example: Brad Pitt was a blond in his latest movie.

Example: Angelina Jolie was a blonde in her latest movie.

Example: The heiress was a fan of blond furniture.

Burglary vs. Robbery

Generally speaking, a *burglary* occurs when someone enters a building with the intention to commit a crime, usually stealing something. A *robbery* occurs when a person is confronted and the use or threat of violence is part of an effort to steal something from that person.

Example: The man committed burglary by breaking into his neighbor's house and stealing a television set.

Example: The man committed robbery by pointing a gun at a woman and demanding that she hand over her purse.

Complement vs. Compliment

Complement means to support, complete or supplement. It also can mean a full set or complete amount. *Compliment* means to give praise or something that is said in admiration.

Example: The addition is a complement to the original structure.

Example: The mayor gave the new structure a nice compliment.

Destroyed vs. Totally Destroyed vs. Partially Destroyed

Use *destroyed* to mean demolished completely. DO NOT use *totally destroyed*. Destroyed means obliterated. It's redundant to say totally destroyed. For the same reasoning, limit your use of *partially destroyed*. Instead of partially destroyed, consider using partially damaged.

Example: The fire destroyed the historic building.

Example: The fire partially destroyed the historic building.

Example: The fire partially damaged the historic building.

Either Or vs. Neither Nor

Use *either/or* for positive comparisons, options or alternatives. *Either/or* means one or the other, but not both. Use *neither/nor* for negative comparisons, options, or alternatives. *Neither/nor* means that both options mentioned will not work or succeed.

Example: Either the San Diego Padres or the Los Angeles Dodgers will win the pennant.

Example: Neither the San Diego Padres nor the Los Angeles Dodgers will win the pennant.

Entitled vs. Titled

Entitled means the right to do or the right to have. *Titled* means the title given to a book, movie, song, etc. DO NOT use *entitled* to refer to how a book, movie, song, etc. is *titled*.

Example: The author is entitled to reap the monetary benefits of her work.

Example: The book is titled, "How to Live with a Real Jerk."

Ensure vs. Insure vs. Assure

Ensure means to guarantee. *Insure* means to provide actual insurance. DO NOT use *insure* unless you're dealing with actual insurance provided by commercial companies. *Assure* means to give confidence or to make a person sure of something.

Example: The governor wanted to ensure the passage of his budget plan, so he promised not to raise taxes.

Example: It is important to insure your home against possible fire damage.

Example: "I assure you that I have nothing to hide," Sosa said.

Example: The injured quarterback wanted to assure his teammates that he'd be ready to play on Saturday.

Every day vs. Everyday

Use *every day* when you want an adverb to describe how often things occur. Use *everyday* when you want an adjective to describe the frequency of events.

Example: He eats an apple every day.

Example: Eating an apple is an everyday thing for him.

Farther vs. Further

Use *farther* when you're referring to physical distance that can actually be measured. Use *further* to mean more time or to a greater degree.

Example: Tiger Woods hits a golf ball farther than most people.

Example: The senator said he needed to study the matter further.

Fewer vs. Less

Generally, use *fewer* when dealing with individual items. Use *less* when dealing with bulk items or quantities.

Example: Fewer than 100 people showed up for the debate.

Example: The senator had less than $100 in his personal account.

Fiancé vs. Fiancée

Use *fiancé* to refer to a male. Use *fiancée* to refer to a female.

Example: Caden Holtzman is the finacé of Hannah Davis.

Example: Hannah Davis is the fiancée of Caden Holtzman.

Hopefully vs. It Is Hoped

Hopefully is an adverb. It means in a hopeful manner. It describes how something was said or how someone appeared. Generally, it is used incorrectly. DO NOT use *hopefully* when you mean "it is hoped."

Example: "It would be great if I could win the lottery," he said hopefully.

Example: It is hoped that the business won't close.

Example: (wrong) Hopefully, the business won't close.

Example: (wrong) Hopefully, we'll get some rain this week.

Imply vs. Infer

Creators of comments and information *imply* things. Readers and listeners *infer* things from the comments and information provided by others.

Example: The comments were so convoluted, it was difficult to determine what the speaker was trying to imply.

Example: The mayor said it would be difficult to infer many positive aspects from the governor's remarks.

Incident vs. Incidence

An *incident* is an event or an occurrence. *Incidence* refers to the degree, extent or range of an event or occurrence.

Example: An unfortunate incident happened during lunch.

Example: The incidence of car theft is on the rise at Midcity University.

Irregardless vs. Regardless
Irregardless is a redundancy. DO NOT use it. *Regardless* means without regard or in spite of.

Example: Regardless of the dangers, the project will begin next week.

Example: (wrong) Irregardless of the dangers, the project will begin next week.

Its vs It's
Its is a possessive pronoun. Use it to indicate ownership of something. *It's* is a contraction for it is or it has. Always double check whether you can substitute "it is" or "it has" for *it's*. If you can, the apostrophe is correct. If you cannot substitute "it is" or "it has" and still have the sentence make sense, you need to use *its*.

Example: Midcity University has its problems.

Example: It's imperative that Midcity University address its problems.

Example: It's been a dry spring in the Midcity area.

Like vs. As
Like can be used as a preposition to compare nouns and pronouns. It takes an object. *As* can be used as a conjunction to link parts of sentence. It does not take an object.

Example: Stan Davis plays golf like a professional.

Example: Stan Davis plays golf as it should be played.

Lose vs. Loose
Lose is a verb that means to misplace, to be unable to find, to fail to keep, or to fail to win. *Loose* is most often used as an adjective. It means free, not confined, not fastened, not tight, or not exact.

Example: It is easy to lose track of time when you're doing something you enjoy.

Example: Did the Padres lose another game?

Example: The suspect was wearing a loose-fitting sweatshirt.

Example: You can't let your dog run loose in the park.

Example: If you let your dog run loose in the park, you might lose it.

Over vs. More Than
Over should be used to describe spatial relationships. *More than* should be used to describe numerical relationships.

Example: A police helicopter hovered over the crime scene.

Example: More than 50 people were injured in the crash.

Example: (wrong) Over 50 people were injured in the crash.

People vs. Persons

Use people when more than one person is involved in something. DO NOT use persons unless it is part of a direct quotation or part of an official title.

Example: More than 250,000 people watched the parade.

Example: (wrong) More than 250,000 persons watched the parade

Example: Marianne Albert is the new director of the Department of Missing Persons.

Principle vs. Principal

A *principle* is a main law, guideline, doctrine or guiding ideal. A *principal* is a ranking authority. *Principal* can also be used as adjective meaning first or foremost.

Example: An important principle of journalism is to strive for accuracy.

Example: Tammy Davis is the principal of Balboa Elementary School.

Example: The principal reason for trading Johnson was to reduce payroll.

Example: Lt. Leonard McFadden is the principal investigator in the case.

Sight vs. Site vs. Cite

Sight has to do with vision. A *site* is a location. A *cite* or *citation* is the bibliographic information about where a quote or passage can be found. *Cite* also can mean to name or refer to.

Example: It's important not to lose sight of your children at a playground.

Example: You're a sight for sore eyes.

Example: The cat was quite a sight after she fell into the pond.

Example: The budget has been approved, but a site for the new gym has not been found.

Example: It's almost impossible to find a downtown building site now.

Example: The professor was not familiar with a cite that Kim included in her research paper.

Example: "Can you cite a credible source for the information you just gave?" Carr asked.

Then vs. Than

Then is an adverb that means at that time, next in time or order, therefore, or besides. *Than* is a conjunction used in comparisons or exceptions.

Example: When Eric finishes his homework, then we'll be able to go to the mall.

Example: First came the rain, and then came the flooding.

Example: If you've read the book, then you'll understand what I'm saying about the movie.

Example: Murphy's debt was larger than Johnson's debt.

Example: "I don't want anything from you other than your friendship," Wicks said.

There vs. Their vs. They're
There is an adverb that is used to indicate direction. *There* also can be used like a pronoun in sentences where the subject of the sentence follows the verb. *Their* is a possessive pronoun. *They're* is a contraction for they are.

Example: The group visited there last summer.

Example: There were no injuries reported.

Example: The students had their books stolen from their dorm rooms.

Example: They're hoping to get reimbursed for the expenses they incurred.

To vs. Too vs. Two
To can be used as part of a direction, part of an infinitive or for a variety of uses when *too* or *two* would not be appropriate. *Too* means more than enough, extremely, or in addition. *Two* is used to express the numeral between one and three.

Example: His boss told him to go to the office supply store.

Example: He had made way too many mistakes to keep his job.

Example: Maxwell said she wanted to attend the concert, too.

Example: The two leading candidates will debate the issues Saturday night.

Under vs. Less Than
Under should be used to express spatial relationships. *Less than* should be used when you're dealing with numbers.

Example: The gun was found under the living room couch.

Example: Officials expect a crowd of less than 30,000 for tonight's game.

Example: (wrong) Officials expect of crowd of under 30,000 for tonight's game.

Who vs. Whom
Who is a pronoun used for references to humans or animals and serves as the subject of a sentence, clause or phrase. *Whom* is a pronoun used for references to humans or animals and serves as the object of a verb or preposition.

Example: The judge wanted to know who was going to guard the prisoner.

Example: Kai was the name of the dog who saved the boy from downing.

Example: Hemingway wanted to know for whom the bell tolls.

Example: "Whom did McMahill hit with the pitch?" the manager asked.

Who's vs. Whose
   Who's is a contraction for who is or who has. *Whose* is a possessive pronoun. If you can't substitute "who is" or "who has" for *who's*, then use *whose*.

Example: Who's the headliner for the concert tomorrow?

Example: Who's got the solution to our money problems?

Example: Whose book was found in the restroom?

Your vs. You're vs. Yore
   Your is the possessive form meaning belonging to you. *You're* is a contraction for you are. If you can't substitute "you are" for *you're*, then use *your*. Yore means long ago. It's not used very often, but when it is, its most often used as the object of the preposition "of."

Example: Your water bills will be going up next month.

Example: You're going to be paying more for water next month.

Example: In days of yore, no one had to pay for water.

Write About It

List FIVE other word usage problems that online newswriters might face.

1.

2.

3.

4.

5.

SECTION FOUR

Legal and Ethical Concerns

Legal and ethical issues surface regularly for online news writers. Among the most common are libel, invasion of privacy, copyright infringement, plagiarism, fabrication, sensationalism and conflicts of interest. It is important for writers to have a basic understanding of how to handle sensitive material and how to avoid getting into legal or ethical trouble.

LIBEL

Defamation is the heart of libel. Defamation occurs when a person's reputation is damaged by false communication that is "printed" about him or her. Defamation occurs when false information causes a person to be hated, shunned, ridiculed or laughed at.

Clearly, the truth or falsity of the information presented is key. Every effort should be made to ensure that the information that is being shared with the public is factual, accurate, fair and balanced. If something doesn't seem right to you, check it out. Take the time to confirm allegations. Be sure you're reporting facts.

Choose your words carefully when dealing with crimes, business dealings and allegations about unethical or unprofessional behavior. Be sure you have the evidence to support charges and allegations. Confirm such things with law enforcement officers, legislative officials and other proper authorities BEFORE putting them online.

Whenever you're tempted to use such words as robber, murderer, child molester, stalker, rapist, drug dealer, bid-rigger, tax cheat, swindler or other derogatory terms, be sure you can defend yourself and your news organization if you're sued for libel. Be sure you can prove the truthfulness of your claims.

Remember, in most cases, if a libel occurs in a story that you write, you and your news organization can be held liable. It really doesn't matter where you obtained the information you used to craft your story, so get into the habit of confirming and verifying any potentially defamatory charges and allegations. Take nothing for granted. Check things out. Obtain the evidence you'll need to defend yourself and your news organization in a court of law and in the court of public opinion.

Take care at all times, but take special care whenever you have one of the following situations:

1. A person is accused of or linked to a crime or to a group associated with criminal activity.

2. A person is accused of or linked to a group associated with a scam, fraud, swindle, or other malfeasance.

3. A person is accused of or linked to a group associated with some sort of racial, ethnic or religious intolerance.

4. A person is accused of being in or linked to a group associated with financial trouble.

5. A person is accused of having a contagious, loathsome and/or socially unacceptable disease.

You should see "red flags" whenever you're tempted to use one or more of the following words, terms or phrases: abortion, abuse, addict, adultery, AIDS, alcoholic, Alzheimer's, arrested, bankrupt, bisexual, bribery, charged, cheat, con artist, convicted, corrupt, crazy, criminal, crook, delinquent, drunk, drug dealer, drug user, DUI, fired, gang member, gay, guilty, HIV positive, illegal, incompetent, insolvent, liar, malpractice, mentally ill, molester, overdose, paranoid, payoff, pervert, racist, rip-off, scam, suicide, thief, traitor, unethical, weird.

Despite your best efforts to report the truth accurately and fairly, it's possible that you might still be sued for libel. If so, there are a variety of defenses that you can use to protect yourself and your news organization.

Truth is the best defense. If you can prove the veracity of what you've reported in your story, you'll likely win the lawsuit.

Fair and accurate reports of what is said and what is done during official proceedings can be shared with the public even if false allegations are made during such proceedings. Testimony and actions during official trials, meetings and hearings can be reported even if the testimony and actions might be potentially defamatory. The content of official documents can be reported as well. Testimony, actions and documents that occur or are obtained outside of the "official" trials, meetings and hearings do not qualify for the special protection of "privilege," though.

When something is offered to the public—a book, a movie, a television program, a concert, a CD, a play, a symphony, a painting, a sculpture, an athletic event—news organizations have a right to comment on and criticize the creative work or performance. As long as the information contained in the story or review is fair and accurate and based on what has been offered to and seen by the public, reasonable protection is provided. Speculation about why a creative work or performance might be inferior or have problems usually does not get the same protection.

Write About It

List FIVE things online news writers can do to help avoid getting themselves and their news organizations involved in libel lawsuits.

1.

2.

3.

4.

5.

INVASION OF PRIVACY

A person's privacy can be invaded in four major ways. A person's physical solitude can be invaded. Private, embarrassing personal facts about a person can be revealed. A person can be put in a false light in the public's eye. Finally, a person's likeness or endorsement can be "misappropriated."

Online news writers normally wouldn't be involved in the invasion of a person's physical solitude, but writers should be on the lookout for examples of potential invasions of physical solitude. Examples include the use of hidden cameras or microphones to obtain information and going onto private property to obtain information without permission. Information gathered about public people in public places or from public records normally is reasonably safe to report.

Online news writers easily can be guilty of one of the other areas associated with invasions of privacy. Take care when reporting old facts, stories and anecdotes that might prove embarrassing for a person. Dredging up such things must be done for good reasons, for "good motives." Be sure that if dirt is being dug up and mud is being slung around, you have a good reason for doing so.

It also is relatively easy to put a person in a "false light" in the public's eye. Misidentifications, incorrect linkages, exaggerations, embellishments and fabrications can give the wrong impression about a person. Online news writers must take great care to be sure that in the heat of battle, mistakes of omission and mistakes of commission are avoided or at least minimized. Report the facts. Don't report rumors. Be careful with speculations.

Online news writers should be sure that endorsements are accurate. Often, people or organizations will suggest they have the endorsements of well-known, influential actors, athletes, legislators and other notables in an effort to make themselves look better and appear more important. Be sure such endorsements have been offered. Avoid misappropriation by validating what people and organizations claim have been said about them by others.

Write About It

List FIVE things online news writers can do to help avoid getting themselves and their news organizations involved in invasion of privacy lawsuits.

1.

2.

3.

4.

5.

COPYRIGHT INFRINGEMENT

If online news writers use their own words to tell their stories, they should not have to worry too much about copyright infringement. Problems come when writers borrow too heavily from source copy, especially source copy that has been crafted by other journalists. Copyright protects the rights of creative people so they can profit from the way they put words together to share information with others. If someone borrows too much of a copyrighted work, he or she can be sued for copyright infringement.

An important thing for online news writers to remember is that facts cannot be copyrighted. The way facts are reported, though, can be, and often is, copyrighted. An author's style, technique, tone and manner of expression are all protected. Again, if an online news writer does his or her own work, copyright concerns should not be an issue very often.

Online news writers can borrow from copyrighted material under what is known as the "Doctrine of Fair Use." The five major aspects of the doctrine include the purpose of the borrowing, the nature of the original work, the amount of material borrowed, the potential financial impact on the original work, and the importance of the issues at stake.

If the borrowing occurs for legitimate news-reporting purposes, writers get a bit of leeway when it comes to using information contained in copyrighted materials. Works of non-fiction that are no longer for sale can be borrowed from a bit more than works of fiction that are still commercially available. Only small amounts of copyrighted material can be borrowed. Avoid lifting entire paragraphs or even entire sentences. A sentence fragment or a phrase or two should be the limit. If what is borrowed reduces the profitability of the original work, a writer might be guilty of copyright infringement. Finally, the event or issue being reported must be highly significant and in the public interest to justify borrowing from copyrighted material. If the public's right to know is not great enough, a writer could lose a copyright infringement lawsuit.

Write About It

List FIVE things online news writers can do to help avoid getting themselves and their news organizations involved in copyright infringement lawsuits.

1.

2.

3.

4.

5.

PLAGIARISM

Even if the "Doctrine of Fair Use" might protect some liberal borrowing from copyrighted works, online news writers should take great care not to plagiarize from the works of others. Even if the liberal borrowing is judged not to be a crime, it is still an egregious breach of professional ethics. Online news writers should not take the work of others and try to pass it off as their own.

Of course, when an online news writer does borrow material from a source, he or she should include attribution to let readers know where the material came from. And, even then, keep the borrowing to a minimum and tell the story in your own words. Don't use the same words as the original author.

Example: According to a report in the *Washington Post*, Sen. Jenkins hired Fleischman to serve as a "special consultant" for the upcoming campaign.

FABRICATION

Making something up is an equally egregious breach of professional ethics. If you don't know something and you can't find the information you need, hold the story if you can or let your readers know that you have an information gap. Don't guess, speculate or fabricate. Don't make up quotes. Newswriting means reporting facts not fictions.

Example: No exact reports on the number of injuries. Reporters are still on the scene attempting to find out how many people might have been hurt.

SENSATIONALISM

Sadly, some journalists and journalistic organizations feel the need to heighten the drama of their stories by sensationalizing events and issues. Avoid the temptation to milk emotions, fears, prejudices, biases and misconceptions. Stick to the documented facts. Don't dwell on gory details or lurid accounts. Sex, crime and violence will always be newsworthy, but you don't have to sensationalize such things. Play it straight. Let the facts speak for themselves. Let your readers decide how to feel about issues and events for themselves. Let the natural drama, emotion and excitement of issues and events attract readership. Don't hype. Don't embellish. Don't exaggerate. Don't sensationalize.

CONFLICTS OF INTEREST

Conflicts of interest can be relatively common in online newswriting. You might have a financial interest in a business that is in the news. You might belong to an organization that is in the news. A group you support might be in the news. You might have a part-time job with a company that is in the news. You might have family members or friends who are in the news.

Whenever you encounter a possible conflict of interest, talk to your editor about it. If possible, you should NOT write a story when a potential conflict of interest exists. If you must write the story, try even harder than normal to be impartial, fair and balanced in your approach to the story. Ask a colleague to check your story for any real or perceived evidence that you might have been influenced by your association with the people, places, issues or things involved in the story.

Real or perceived conflicts of interest can undermine the all-important credibility that online news organizations must have to succeed. Even though total objectivity is almost never possible, it is a good goal or ideal. At least try to be as objective as you can, especially when you're faced with potential financial or allegiance-oriented conflicts of interest.

Write About It

Why is it so important for online news writers to guard against plagiarism, fabrication, sensationalism and conflicts of interest?

CODES OF ETHICS

The guidelines contained in the ethics codes of journalistic organizations and associations can be helpful when online news writers are confronted with ethical dilemmas. The Society of Professional Journalists and the Radio-Television News Directors Association both have well-respected ethics codes. Highlights include the following:

1. Seek the truth and provide fair, comprehensive accounts of significant events and issues.

2. Be thorough in news gathering, reporting and writing.

3. Be honest.

4. Confirm the accuracy of information obtained from ALL sources.

5. **Do not** misrepresent the comments, beliefs, attitudes, values and behaviors of sources.

6. Guard against the oversimplification of events and issues.

7. Remain impartial.

8. Avoid stereotyping people by race, gender, age, religion, ethnicity, geography, sexual orientation, disability, physical appearance or social status.

9. Provide a context for facts and figures. Report the meaning associated with events and issues.

10. **Do not** pander to lurid curiosity.

11. Hold government and business leaders accountable for their actions.

12. Emphasize the significance, relevance and importance of events and issues.

13. **Do not** plagiarize.

14. Avoid conflicts of interest.

15. Correct mistakes promptly and completely.

All journalistic codes of ethics stress a few core values. These values help define responsible journalism and can be used by journalists in their efforts to practice their profession in an ethical manner. The values include the following:

1. Serve the public and defend the public's right to know.

2. Seek and report the truth, but do so in a manner that provides meaning.

3. Be fair and impartial.

4. Report the significance and relevance of events and issues.

5. Avoid conflicts of interest and respect the dignity and intelligence of news consumers and news sources.

6. Remain independent and resist the influence of those who strive to control news content.

7. Be accountable for your actions.

Visit the web sites of the Society of Professional Journalists, the Radio-Television News Directors Association, the Poynter Institute and the Project for Excellence in Journalism and the Committee of Concerned Journalists often. You'll find a great deal of valuable, useful information, tips and suggestions for improving skills, performance and ethics.

http://www.spj.org
http://www.rtnda.org
http://www.poynter.org
http://www.journalism.org

Another useful web site for online news writers is http://www.cyberjournalist.net

Write About It

Suggest FIVE additional ethical guidelines that online news writers should follow. Why do you feel the way you do?

1.

2.

3.

4.

5.

Style Tests and Writing Exercises

STYLE TESTS

Style Test 1

Write the following in correct online newswriting style. Assume each item appears in the middle of a sentence. If an item is correct as written, place an X in the blank.

1. 33% _____

2. one-thousand-two hundred _____

3. fifteen million dollars _____

4. seven-hundred-68 _____

5. five p.m. in the evening _____

6. November 6, 2007 _____

7. 641 _____

8. 25¢ _____

9. four _____

10. 13,892 _____

Style Test 2

Write the following in correct online newswriting style. Assume each item appears in the middle of a sentence. If an item is correct as written, place an X in the blank.

1. 8% _____

2. 2,000 _____

3. $5.2 billion _____

4. 4-hundred-44 _____

5. 9 this morning _____

6. Apr. 26 1976 _____

7. 3 cents _____

8. 20 dollars _____

9. nineteen _____

10. 6-thousand-twenty-three _____

Style Test 3

Write the following in correct online newswriting style. Assume each item appears in the middle of a sentence. If an item is correct as written, place an X in the blank.

1. 25-hundred lbs. _____

2. thirteen in. _____

3. 6 ft. _____

4. twenty oz. _____

5. 150 yards _____

6. 2 ltr. _____

7. 8 mm film _____

8. 955 mi. _____

9. forty acres _____

10. 16 millimeters _____

Style Test 4

Write the following in correct online newswriting style. Assume each item appears in the middle of a sentence. If an item is correct as written, place an X in the blank.

1. 45 square in. _____

2. ninety sq. feet _____

3. two quarts _____

4. 60 kilometers _____

5. one-hundred-ten meters _____

6. seventy-five square yds. _____

7. 39 centimeters _____

8. sixteen tons _____

9. 8 ounces _____

10. eighty-seven gals. _____

Style Test 5

Write the following in correct online newswriting style. Assume each item appears in the middle of a sentence. If an item is correct as written, place an X in the blank.

1. Stanley K. Davis, fifty-five _____

2. 8423 Market Avenue _____

3. Major Monica L. Torres _____

4. CIA _____

5. professor Barbara M. Mueller _____

6. Sergeant Alexander A. Asbury _____

7. 697 Nile Blvd. _____

8. the sixteen-year-old boy _____

9. the 1920's and 1930's _____

10. 4321 Fifty-Seventh St. _____

Style Test 6

Write the following in correct online newswriting style. Assume each item appears in the middle of a sentence. If an item is correct as written, place an X in the blank.

1. Linus V. Chang (Democrat-California) _____

2. Mrs. Nora P. Granger, 32 _____

3. Benjamin K. Valenzuela, Junior _____

4. Super Bowl 40 _____

5. Mon., January 1st _____

6. Ames, Ia. _____

7. Lt. Col. Sean O'Keefe, forty-nine _____

8. the nineteen-year-old girl _____

9. nine-and-1/2 _____

10. two-point-five ft. _____

Style Test 7

Rewrite the following sentences in correct online newswriting style. The sentences are not leads for stories.

1. If the 20% cut is made, ten of the fifty employees will loose there jobs.

2. Your going to be paying at least 3 dollars a gallon for gas soon.

3. The city cannot afford a new library and will not be able to pay it's creditors, Moore said.

4. The brush fire was started by a lightening strike.

5. "Whose responsible for the forty-five-million-dollar debt?" Gonzales asked.

6. Captain Lucinda Maria Munoz will retire in Jan.

7. The damage to the hotel was estimated at one-half-million-dollars by Fire Captain Caitlyn McFadden.

8. The office will be open Mon., Tue., Wed. and Thu. until the end of Jun.

9. A elephant and an giraffe were shipped to the Midcity Zoo by the San Diego Zoo.

10. Mary Zelasko, eighty-three, was injured when a twelve-ft ladder fell on her.

Style Test 8

Rewrite the following sentences in correct online newswriting style. The sentences are not leads for stories.

1. Dr. Diane Borden, a journalism prof. at Midcity University, was awarded a $500,000 grant from the Gannett Foundation.

2. Admiral Elena Vazquez said, "Mr. & Mrs. Simpson were very kind to me in my time of need."

3. "Nearly 1/3 of adult Americans believe in UFOs," said Dr. Jerry D. Greene, Junior.

4. Linda Michelle Salazar, fifty-five, 8921 Tina Ln., died in the crash.

5. "You're a site for sore eyes," Williams said as he hugged his brother.

6. The new building will cost $6,750,000, according to a report by the Midcity Public Works Dept.

7. The recipe called for twelve gals. of ice cream, 2 lbs. of peanuts, sixty-four oz. of whipped cream and two qts. of chocolate syrup.

8. Leonard McFadden, the third, and Leonard McFadden, the fourth, have been charged with felony assault, according to Lieutenant Martha Lowery.

9. The kickoff was supposed to be at seven o'clock tomorrow night, but ESPN requested that the time be moved to six o'clock.

10. Experts predict that students likely will have to pay 25% more for they're books this semester.

Style Test 9

Rewrite the following sentences in correct online newswriting style. The sentences are not leads for stories.

1. "Except my advise and the affect will be minimized," Suzuki said.

2. Governor Sorenson has selected Carolyn Brown, a administrative aid to State Senator Kristin Padilla, as his new exec. asst.

3. Even though she is a alumnus of Midcity University, the blond surfer says the disagreement between the three universities is mostly the fault of Midcity University.

4. Experts say if you want to improve the performance of employees, complement them often and that will insure more productivity and a friendlier office environment.

5. Jackson hoped to travel further into the jungle everyday.

6. The team says it's principle reason for raising ticket prices is increased insurance costs.

7. Their hoping to improve there record by playing smaller schools in the preseason.

8. Harrison wanted too attend the concert, to.

9. The crowd was estimated at over 30-thousand by team officials.

10. Who did the mayor blame for the five-million-dollar budget shortfall?

Style Test 10

Rewrite the following sentences in correct online newswriting style. The sentences are not leads for stories.

1. Under fifty persons attended the first town-hall meeting.

2. "Whose wondering about who's money was stolen?" Albertson asked.

3. "Your going to have to take better care of you're equipment," the coach said.

4. The historic building was totally destroyed in the 3-alarm fire.

5. The play is entitled, "The Last Quarter," and it will begin at 8 o'clock p.m. tonight.

6. In his speech, Copeland inferred that he would run for office irregardless of the embarrassment his family might experience.

7. Its not definite, but the budget could exceed $20,750,000 next year.

8. Nieto weighs more then Simpson, but Simpson should not be effected to much by the weight difference.

9. Running 8 miles is an every day ritual for Whittler.

10. Greene wanted to discuss the matter farther, but Denton had to leave to meet his fiancé, Brenda.

NEWS BRIEFS

Note: Web sites where readers can get additional information are listed at the end of each brief.

News Brief 1

Man Crashes Through Window After Crashing Car Into Tree

Suspected car thief arrested at 3:45 p.m. this afternoon.

Man is suspected of stealing a 2005 Ford Escort from outside a home at 6528 Pine Street.

Midcity police officers chased the man for about 15 miles.

Man drove the stolen car into a tree near 4379 Sunshine Lane. He exited the vehicle and, after a brief sprint across a lawn, dove through the front picture window of the home at 4379 Sunshine Lane.

Midcity police officers surrounded the home and the man surrendered at 5:25 p.m.

John V. Enright, 41, was jailed on suspicion of auto theft, burglary and fleeing police.

Enright suffered multiple lacerations, but none of his injuries is thought to be life-threatening. He was treated at the infirmary at the Midcity County Jail.

No other injuries were reported.

http://www.mpd.gov

News Brief 2

Local Stores Hit by Burglars

Jewelry store on Market Street downtown hit by burglars at 4:30 a.m. this morning.

Burglars used a heavy-duty saw to cut their way into Raul's Discount Jewelry at 2863 Market Street, according to Midcity Police.

Raul J. Conejo, 54, the owner of Raul's Discount Jewelry, estimated that the crooks got away with approximately $255,000 in gold and silver jewelry. Damage to store estimated at $10,000.

A similar saw was used in an aborted attempt to rob another store on Market Street this morning, according to police. Crazy Mike's Electronics was hit about 2:15 a.m., but an alarm apparently scared off the would-be burglars. Damage to store estimated at $7,500.

Police are asking anyone with information about either crime to call (555) 999-9111.

http://www.mpd.gov

News Brief 3

Unknown Illness Kills 17 in China

Unidentified illness has claimed the lives of 17 farmers in southwestern China. 41 other people have been sickened by the same illness.

Authorities in China report that after butchering sick pigs and sheep, the people fell ill yesterday.

Symptoms included high fever, fatigue, nausea, vomiting, headache, blurred vision and chest pains.

After experiencing the symptoms for several hours, the people became comatose and bruises appeared under their skin in several places.

Authorities in China believe a bacterial infection likely is responsible for the deaths and illness.

Chinese authorities do not expect any more people will demonstrate similar symptoms. All of the farmers and others who were involved in the butchering of the sick animals have either died or are already ill. In addition, all of the diseased animals involved in the incident have been destroyed and disposed of.

The disease does not appear to be contagious, according to authorities. It appears that the disease is contracted via direct contact with diseased animals.

http://www.diseasecontrol.org

News Brief 4

Nigerian Bus Accident Kills 56

56 people died when a long-haul passenger bus ran off a bridge and skidded into a river in northern Nigeria this morning.

Law enforcement officials in Kano, Nigeria, reported that the bus driver likely fell asleep at the wheel.

8 people were rescued from the wreckage of the luxury bus.

The bus began its overnight trip in the southern city of Lagos. It ran off the Tamburaw Bridge near Kano.

The bus dropped more than 300 feet.

Most of the survivors had been sitting near the rear of the bus.

Most of the victims died from burns suffered when the bus exploded shortly after impact, according to law enforcement officials.

http://www.nigerianews.com

News Brief 5

Pirate Radio Station Silenced

Free Radio 93.3 FM, an unlicensed radio broadcaster in the Midcity area was shut down at 2:10 this morning. The station uses the call letters PIRAT.

Federal agents, armed with a search warrant, raided the self-proclaimed oldest-operating "pirate" radio station in Midcity.

More than 12 agents from the Federal Communications Commission served the warrant at a home at 8871 Hill Street. The agents seized amplifiers, computers, microphones, a transmitter and other equipment.

Skot S. Norton, 24, who lives in the home at 8871 Hill Street, was taken into custody and charged with operating an unlicensed radio station.

Mark W. Warren, 27, 8873 Hill Street, witnessed the raid.

Quote from Mark W. Warren:

"This is a First Amendment issue. My friends and I are going to raise some money and get some new equipment. We'll get the station back on the air someplace else real soon."

http://www.fcc.gov
http://www.pirat.com

News Brief 6

Midcity School Board Cuts Staff and Hours

Midcity Unified School District Board of Education approved a plan this morning to eliminate 52 classified jobs and reduce the hours of 49 positions.

The vote was 5-4 in favor of the plan.

The cuts will result in a budget savings of $1.5 million.

The cuts were made at schools that have experienced declining enrollments for at least two consecutive years.

Among the workers who will be cut are dozens of office clerks, classroom aides and other support staffers.

Librarians, groundskeepers and janitors will all have their hours cut.

The job eliminations and hour reductions will take effect at the beginning of the next school year.

http://musd.edu

News Brief 7

Fires Ravage Western States

Wild fires raging in four western states.

In Utah, a 18,000-acre fire is threatening several small towns. No evacuations ordered, yet, but officials have warned residents to be ready to evacuate later today. The fire is burning about 40 miles south of Provo.

In Colorado, a fast-moving grass fire has burned 6,500 acres. No structures destroyed. The fire is burning about 50 miles southwest of Denver.

In Arizona, a 70,250-acre fire continues to threaten homes and out buildings. No structures damaged so far. The fire is burning near the central Arizona community of Sunflower.

In California, a 9,750-acre brush fire continued its march toward residential communities. Three homes and several garages destroyed so far. The fire is burning about 35 miles northeast of San Diego.

http://www.bureauoflandmanagement.gov
http://nationalforestservice.gov

News Brief 8

Midcity University Vows Fight Against Grade Inflation

Faculty members at Midcity University voted this afternoon to limit A grades to no more than 35% of the students in each class.

The limit includes A-plus, A and A-minus grades.

A recent study found that on average 46% of the students in each class have received A grades.

In the mid-1980s, about 31% of students received A grades.

The Midcity University plan is modeled after similar quota systems at Princeton University, Harvard University and the University of California campuses.

Quote from Dr. Kona Valenzuela, vice-president for academic affairs, Midcity University:

> Limits on giving A grades have worked at other universities, so we think we can make it work at Midcity University. I think professors will abide by the new guidelines, because every class in every department and school in the university will be following the same rules."

The new grade limits take effect next semester.

http://www.muacademicaffairs.edu

News Brief 9

Midcity Woman Wins Lobster-Eating Contest

Serena Michelle Nixon, 27, ate 39 lobsters in 12 minutes today to win the World Lobster Eating Contest in Kennebunk, Maine.

Nixon won $5,000 and a trophy belt for consuming 10.75 pounds of lobster meat.

Each speed eating contestant had a partner cracking the shells and pulling out the meat.

12 competitors ate 310.56 pounds of the crustaceans during the 12-minute contest.

Nixon stands 5-foot-2 and weighs 110 pounds.

Quote from Serena Nixon:

   "I guess I just have the type of stomach that can handle speed eating. It's fun. I enjoy it."

Last month, Nixon won the World Baked Beans Eating Contest when she consumed 8.8 pounds of baked beans in three minutes.

http://www.speedeating.org

News Brief 10

Bargain Hunters Crush Woman at Discount King Store

A mob of shoppers rushing to grab low-priced DVD players at the Discount King store in West Midcity trampled a woman and knocked her unconscious this morning.

Doris M. McKenzie, 54, 715 Moraga Dr., was vying for one of a limited number of bargained-priced DVD players that had been widely advertised for the past week.

The DVD players were priced at $19.99.

Mrs. McKenzie was first in line when the store opened at 8:00 a.m. When the doors opened, the mass of bargain hunters pushed through the doors. Mrs. McKenzie either lost her balanced or was shoved to the ground and was run over by more than 100 shoppers.

Paramedics were called to the scene and later transported Mrs. McKenzie to Midcity General Hospital.

She was treated for contusions, lacerations, abrasions and a mild concussion.

Douglas P. Dowdy, the manager of the Discount King store, said Mrs. McKenzie would be given a $500 shopping pass and two free DVD players.

http://www.mfd.gov
http://www.discountking.com

CAPTIONS

Picture Caption 1
Write a caption for the described picture in correct online newswriting style.

Picture:

Somewhat blurry shot of U.S. Astronaut Hunter Gardner in a space suit working in the payload bay of the space shuttle Explorer. It is clear Gardner is in outer space.

Information:

U.S. Astronaut Hunter Gardner stepped outside Explorer and made repairs on a broken robot arm this morning. Engineers suspect a lubrication problem with the bearings is the cause of the malfunction. Fellow spacewalker Heather Hernandez snapped the photo of Gardner.

Picture Caption 2
Write a caption for the described picture in correct online newswriting style.

Picture:

A van is shown with all of its windows broken. Severe structural damage is evident. The roof is caved in, doors are twisted and misshapen. The van is leaning against a small hill with two wheels in the air. Two men are carrying a body covered with a sheet away from the van. The body is on a stretcher.

Information:

Fatal crash in North Midcity early this morning. According to Midcity Police Department officials, the driver apparently fell asleep and the van veered off Interstate 15 near the Coyote Canyon off-ramp. The van rolled over several times as it slipped down a small incline and rolled over up against a small hill. 6 people killed and 3 people injured. The 3 injured people are in "critical" condition.

Map Caption 1

Write a caption for the described map in correct online newswriting style.

Map:

Street grid with several labeled roads. High Mesa Blvd. runs near top of map. Little Creek Rd. runs near bottom of map. Park Blvd. runs up the left side of the map. Crest Ln. runs down the right side of the map. A large, black square is visible in the upper left corner. The words "Future site of George W. Bush Elementary School" appear near the black square.

Information:

Construction has been delayed on the $16.5 million George W. Bush Elementary School. Environmentalists say the site is the home for many endangered species of plants and birds. Construction was scheduled to begin this morning, but a Superior Court judge has issued a temporary restraining order halting the project. Experts say legal challenges could delay the project for more than 2 years. Such a delay would add at least $4 million to the price tag for the project.

Map Caption 2

Write a caption for the described map in correct online newswriting style.

Map:

Street grid of entire city. 5 large colored circles dot the map. The number 1 is inside the red dot. The number 2 is inside the blue dot. The number 3 is inside the green dot. The number 4 is inside the yellow dot. The number 5 is inside the orange dot. Several streets are labeled.

Information:

Midcity University's Department of Urban Planning has issued a report about the most dangerous intersections in the city. Data collected for the past 5 years. All traffic accidents in which police units responded were included in the study.

Red Dot: The most dangerous intersection is the corner of Highdale Rd. and Mast Blvd. in North Midcity. 210 accidents.

Blue Dot: The second most dangerous intersection is the corner of Mountain Pass Dr. and College St. in West Midcity. 193 accidents.

Green Dot: The third most dangerous intersection is the corner of Virginia St. and Tennessee Dr. in South Midcity. 184 accidents.

Yellow Dot: The fourth most dangerous intersection is the corner of Western Blvd. and Wagner Way in East Midcity. 177 accidents.

Orange Dot: The fifth most dangerous intersection is the corner of Oak St. and Maple St. in North Midcity. 158 accidents.

Chart Caption 1

Write a caption for the described chart in correct online newswriting style.

Chart:

Shows 6 black bars of different heights. A month is listed under each bar. At the top of the chart are the words, "Violent Crime in Midcity." For the Jan. bar, the number 16 rests at the top. For the Feb. bar, the number 13 rests at the top. For the Mar. bar, the number 18 rests at the top. For the Apr. bar, the number 21 rests at the top. For the May bar, the number 11 rests at the top. For the Jun. bar, the number 9 rests at the top.

Information:

The Midcity Police Department has released latest crime statistics—months of Jan.-Jun. Violent crime actually down about 12% from the same period last year. Violent crime includes assaults and murders.

Jan: 16 cases; Feb: 13 cases; Mar: 18 cases; Apr: 21 cases; May: 11 cases; Jun: 9 cases

Chart Caption 2

Write a caption for the described chart in correct online newswriting style.

Chart:

Pie chart divided into three sections of different colors. Largest section is red. Second largest is blue. Third largest is yellow. The words, "Professional Schools Scholarships," are inside the blue section. The words, "Undergraduate Scholarships," are inside the red section. The words, "Graduate Program Scholarships," are inside the yellow section.

Information:

Midcity University released its proposed scholarship budget for next year. The university reports that it needs $5.25 million to fund undergraduate student scholarships. It needs $4.33 million to fund scholarships for students in the university's professional schools—law, medicine and veterinary. It needs $3.85 million to fund scholarships for graduate students. The $13.43 million total is a 5.5% increase over last year. Tuition was raised 10% this year from what it cost last year.

AUDIO CUTS

Audio Cut Introduction 1

Write an introduction to the audio cut in correct online newswriting style.

Audio Cut From Supervisor Roger Hedgeman:

"I've never knowingly accepted money from anyone in exchange for a political favor. I haven't done anything that every other supervisor hasn't done."

Information:

Midcity Board of Supervisor Roger Hedgeman is accused of accepting a bribe from a local land developer.

Hedgeman accused of accepting $50,000 from Karl M. Kemper, 53, 6219 Rancho Santa Fe Dr.

Kemper allegedly gave Hedgeman the $50,000 in exchange for Hedgeman's help in convincing the Board of Supervisors to change the zoning on a 45-acre parcel of land that Kemper owns in East Midcity. Kemper wants to build condominiums and townhouses on the property, but current zoning regulations call for single-family homes only.

The vote on the zoning change has been suspended pending the outcome of the case against Hedgeman.

Audio Cut Introduction 2

Write an introduction to the audio cut in correct online newswriting style.

Audio Cut From State Sen. Edward Murray:

"This is a great day for Midcity. It's taken a little longer than we'd planned, but the wait was worth it. This is a wonderful facility. It should really help the community."

Information:

The South Midcity Recreation Center dedicated this afternoon.

St. Sen. Edward Murray sponsored the bill in the state legislature that provided the money for the recreation center.

The $20.5 million project took two years to complete. It was on the drawing boards for about five years. First three years featured legal battles over land acquisition, zoning and construction bids. Actual construction took two years.

The 2-story recreation center includes the following facilities:

Basketball/volleyball gymnasium—2 courts
Olympic-size swimming pool
Exercise/weight rooms
Indoor running track
Restrooms
Showers
Whirlpool spas

Mayor Ronald Moore and all the members of the Midcity Board of Supervisors attended dedication ceremony. St. Sen. Edward Murray served as "master of ceremonies."

The South Midcity Recreation Center will open to the public tomorrow at 9:00 a.m.

Hours will be 9:00 a.m.-10:00 p.m. daily.

VIDEO PACKAGES

Reporter Video Package Introduction 1

Write an introduction for the reporter package in correct online newswriting style. None of the information provided is in the reporter's package.

Beginning Of Reporter Package:

"The nurses are upset about the hospital's latest salary offer. Union leaders say they're prepared to strike for as long as it takes to get what they deserve."

Information:

Nurses at Midcity General Hospital are on strike. Nurses walking picket line in front of the hospital. They started picketing at 6:00 a.m.

The hospital's management team has offered the nurses a 4% raise, but the nurses want a 6% raise.

The average salary for nurses at Midcity General Hospital is $60,500.

All of the 240 nurses at Midcity General are members of the Midcity Nurses Association.

The hospital is staying open using per diem nurses and management personnel, but the emergency room has been closed. Emergency cases are being diverted to Midcity Community Hospital.

Reporter Juanita Castillo met with representatives of the nurse's union and the hospital's management team. In the video, she is seen talking with a variety of people while picketers march by her with signs. Nurses and supporters can be heard chanting "Two percent more, two percent more," during most of the video.

Reporter Video Package Introduction 2

Write an introduction for the reporter package in correct online newswriting style. None of the information provided is in the reporter's package.

Beginning Of Reporter Package:

"As you can see from the pizza sauce all over my face and shirt, the pizza was flying fast and furious today at Kennedy Park. I tried my best, but I finished a distant fifth in the Senior Division's Pizza Eating Contest."

Information:

Speed-eating contests all day at Kennedy Park in West Midcity.

Contests included the following:

Pizza
Ice cream
Hot dogs
Corn on the cob
Baked beans

Three age groups for all contests—teenagers, 20-50 year olds, and seniors.

Contests sponsored by the Midcity Parks and Recreation Association. It was the second annual "Midcity Speed Eating Festival."

All food donated by local merchants and business owners.

Crowd estimated at 5,000.

About 175 competitors took part.

Reporter Carl Carpenter covered the event. He even entered the pizza-eating contest, senior division. Video begins with Carpenter looking into camera and talking about his contest. Other competitors can be seen behind him. They're using towels to wipe their faces, hands and arms.

VIDEO SCRIPTS

Video Script 1

Write a video script in correct online newswriting style from the provided shot list.

Shot List:

1. Cover shot of firefighters, house and flames :06
2. Close-up of Capt. McFadden :06
3. Close-up of blackened bed frame :06
4. Medium shot of firefighters carrying cats :06
5. Cover shot of fire trucks and smoking house :06

Information:

Fire in East Midcity this morning. House at 8752 Tina Way fully involved when firefighters arrived.

Quote from Capt. Caitlyn S. McFadden, Midcity Fire Department:

"It looks as if the fire started in the master bedroom. The owner says he was burning some candles near the bed and fell asleep. From the looks of the bed frame, I'd say the candles ignited the bed sheets and then spread to the rest of the house. The guy was lucky his smoke detector worked well and he was able to get out alive."

Owner of the house: Franklin H. Schwartz, 69. He is a retired postal worker.

Schwartz breeds cats as a home-based business. Firefighters were able to rescue 53 cats and kittens, but another 29 died in the fire.

McFadden estimated damage to the house, which was totally destroyed, and it's contents at $425,000.

Firefighters received call at 3:45 a.m. They were on the scene until 8:15 a.m.

Fire contained to the house. A detached garage was not damaged.

No injuries reported.

Quote from Franklin Schwartz:

"I guess the fire was my fault. I was just trying to save a little money on electricity. I've used candles before and nothing bad happened. I just hate it that some of my cats didn't make it. I'm sick about it."

Video Script 2

Write a video script in correct online newswriting style from the provided shot list.

Shot List:

1.	Cover shot of damaged truck and car	:06
2.	Medium shot of covered bodies	:06
3.	Close-up shot of Sgt. Connors	:03
4.	Medium shot of tow truck loading the pickup truck	:06
5.	Medium shot of Ozzie Lambert	:06
6.	Cover shot of tow truck leaving scene	:03

Information:

Fatal traffic accident during morning rush hour today. 2 people died in the accident.

Vehicles involved: 2005 Ford F-150 pickup truck; 2006 Dodge Neon.

Crash occurred at 7:30 a.m. at the corner of Clear Springs Dr. and Palm Ave. in West Midcity.

Victims: Douglas M. Maxwell, 34, 274 Valley View St., and Kathrine D. Simmons, 31, 5177 Perkins Blvd.

Both victims worked at The Tool Warehouse in West Midcity. They were on their way to work at the time of the crash.

Simmons was the driver of the Neon. Maxwell was a passenger in her car.

The driver of the F-150 was Ozzie Lambert, 26, 443 Baxter Ln. He was the only person in the truck. He was not injured.

Lambert works at The Tool Warehouse, too.

Quote from Sgt. Charles Connors, Midcity Police Dept.:

"We think the driver of truck ran a stop sign and smashed into the side of the Dodge. He says his accelerator got stuck. We're going to conduct a thorough investigation."

Truck taken to the police impound lot for a forensic investigation.

Quote from Ozzie Lambert:

"My truck just took off. I didn't even press on the gas pedal that hard. I tried to brake, but it was too late. I know those people. I work with them. I'm devastated. I'm so, so sorry, but it wasn't my fault."

Sgt. Connors estimates that the investigation will take at least a week and maybe as much as two weeks to complete.

No charges have been filed against Lambert.

NEWS STORIES

Note: Web sites where readers can get additional information are listed at the end of each story.

News Story 1

Americans Living Longer

Life expectancy for Americans is now 77.6 years.

Declines in death rates from most major causes—heart disease, cancer, diabetes, stroke, respiratory disease, flu and pneumonia, accidents and suicide—have pushed life expectancy to a record high.

Women are still living longer than men, but difference is not as great as it used to be.

Women's life expectancy = 80.1 years.

Men's life expectancy = 74.8 years.

Gap between life expectancy for women and men has been steadily declining since the peak difference year of 1979 when the difference was 7.8 years.

"Research shows that Americans are not only living longer, but they are also leading more active lives," said Dr. Melissa Valenzuela, a sociology professor at Midcity University. "We really don't have a lot of very old, sick people. Most of our seniors are extremely active and continue to make important contributions."

Despite the improvements in the life expectancy rates in the United States, Americans continue to trail other countries, according to statistics provided by the World Health Organization.

Japan ranks number one in the world with an average life expectancy of 81.9 years.

Monaco ranks number two at 81.2 years. San Marino and Switzerland are at 80.6. Australia stands at 80.4. Andorra has a rate of 80.3, and Iceland has a rate of 80.1.

Other countries with higher life expectancy rates than the United States include the following: Austria, Belgium, Canada, Finland, France, Germany, Greece, Israel, Italy, Luxembourg, Malta, Netherlands, New Zealand, Norway, Singapore, Spain and the United Kingdom.

United States-based information from the National Center for Health Statistics.

http://www.nchs.org
http://www.musociology.edu

News Story 2

Chimps Injure Two People Near Fresno

Two people seriously injured today in an attack by two chimpanzees.

Chimpanzees shot dead by sheriff's deputies and animal control officers.

Attack happened at the "Back to the Wild Animal Haven."

Several chimpanzees broke out of their cages at the animal sanctuary near Fresno, California, and attacked some visitors.

One of the injured persons was airlifted to Fresno Memorial Hospital. He suffered injuries to his face, hands, feet and groin. He is in critical condition.

The other person was taken by ambulance to the same hospital with bite wounds to her hand. She is in serious condition.

Injured man identified as Martin Terence Boyd, 52, of Bakersfield, California.

Injured woman identified as Joyce Anne Boyd, 50, also of Bakersfield. She is the wife of Mr. Boyd. They have been married for 30 years.

Mr. and Mrs. Boyd were visiting the sanctuary to celebrate the birthday of Monty, an orphaned chimpanzee they had rescued several years earlier during a trip to Africa.

According to Sgt. Lawrence Sweet of the Fresno County Sheriff's Department, Mr. Boyd had brought a banana cake for Monty, but as he approached the chimpanzee enclosure, two other chimpanzees, Oliver and Brady, attacked him.

Dr. Sandra McFadden, of Fresno Memorial Hospital, said the chimps bit off all of Mr. Boyd's fingers, one of his ears, and his nose. In addition, Dr. McFadden reported Mr. Boyd suffered serious wounds to one of his feet and to his groin area.

Mrs. Boyd had her left thumb bitten off, according to Dr. McFadden.

"The injuries to Mr. Boyd are extensive and very serious," Dr. McFadden said. "It will take many hours of delicate surgery to try to restore Mr. Boyd to any form of normalcy."

Oliver and Brady were shot and killed after the 10 a.m. attack. Two other chimpanzees that had also escaped were returned to their enclosure. Monty never left the enclosure and was not involved in the attack.

Workers at the "Back to the Wild Animal Haven" are not sure how the chimpanzees escaped, but they are investigating. Sheriff's officers are investigating as well.

The "Back to the Wild Animal Haven" has held state permits to shelter animals since 1976. It serves as a sanctuary for exotic animals that have been confiscated or donated.

The "Back to the Wild Animal Haven" permits are held by Roger and Lucinda Morgan. Neither could be reached for comment.

Source for most of the information: Sgt. Lawrence Sweet, Fresno County Sheriff's Department.

http://www.fresnosheriff.gov
http://www.midcityzoo.org

News Story 3

Midcity University Frosh Need Remediation

39% of freshmen entering Midcity University this year need remedial help academically.

MU's Department of Institutional Research released report today.

The students are not ready for college-level writing and math.

Five years ago, Midcity University established a goal of having 90% of its incoming freshmen qualified to immediately begin college-level work in writing and math.

No significant improvement in college readiness has been documented in the past five years, despite the investment of more than $15,000,000 in new textbooks, special programs, teacher-training sessions and increased testing in middle schools and high schools throughout the state.

Quote from Dr. Sandra Michaels, dean of admissions, Midcity University:

"We're disappointed, of course. I'm sure middle school and high school teachers are doing the best they can, but when students aren't prepared for college-level work, it puts a tremendous amount of pressure on us to offer remediation opportunities. For every dollar we have to spend on remediation, it's a dollar we can't spend on enhancement or required courses and programs. We're not giving up, though, and I'm sure state education officials are still committed to doing what's necessary to get students ready to enter college. It's just going to take some more time."

MU spends about $2,000,000 per year on remedial programs in writing and math.

MU offers semester-long courses, workshops, tutors and self-directed learning programs for students who need remedial work in writing and math.

MU requires that prospective freshmen take two qualifying tests during the first semester of their senior year in high school. Scores on the Writing Assessment Test and the Math Assessment Test are used to determine whether a student is ready for college-level writing assignments and mathematics courses. A student must score a 70 out of a possible 100 on each examination to be judged ready for college-level work.

Quote from Dr. Hector Munoz, director of university advancement, Midcity University:

"We're hoping to enlist the support of local businesses and organizations to help us provide more resources for middle schools and high schools in the state. In addition, we want to raise money to help fund special programs in the summer so students who need some remediation can get it prior to beginning their regular college work. We're very optimistic that business and community leaders will step up and help us meet this critical need in higher education."

http://www.muadmissions.edu

News Story 4

Obesity Can Shorten Life Span

New report from researchers at Midcity University's School of Public Health released today.

Obesity is eroding the gains Americans have made in extending their life spans. If current trends continue, obesity likely will halt the long trend toward increasing longevity.

Researchers say Americans must take aggressive steps to reduce their weight.

Illnesses caused by obesity are currently reducing the average U.S. life span by at least five to ten months.

Quote from Dr. Leland Chang, professor, School of Public Health, Midcity University:

"In the next 50 years or so, if Americans don't reverse the trend toward obesity, the average life span will be cut by almost five years. Clearly, we must do all we can to get the message out that being overweight can have serious negative impacts on health and life expectancy."

According to researchers, obesity can lead to increased chances of contracting diabetes, heart disease and cancer.

The researchers claim at least 66% of Americans are overweight including at least 33% who are obese.

The researchers based their calculations on statistics gathered by the National Center for Health Statistics.

Quote from Dr. Maria Gonzales, professor of demography, School of Public Health, Midcity University:

"We're really concerned about the growing rate of obesity in children. We found that almost 25% of American children can be called obese today and there are no signs that things are going to get any better any time soon. As a country, we have to get more serious about being sure we eat right, reduce our daily intake of calories and get sufficient exercise. If we don't, the health and economic implications are mind-boggling. We could be heading for a nationwide health disaster."

http://www.muschoolofpublichealth.edu
http://www.nchs.org

News Story 5

Capital Punishment Banned for Youths

WASHINGTON—The U.S. Supreme Court, believing that America and the world have turned against the death penalty for youthful offenders, ruled this morning that the U.S. Constitution bans capital punishment for crimes committed by persons under the age of 18.

The 6-3 decision, which upheld a ruling by the Mississippi Supreme Court, will immediately remove 62 persons in 12 states off of death row. The ruling stated that execution of persons who kill at an age younger than 18 violates the Eighth Amendment's prohibition against "cruel and unusual punishments."

Writing for the court, Justice Anthony Mendoza said the decision was necessary to be in line with the "evolving standards of decency" that have shaped the Supreme Court's view of what constitutes cruel and unusual punishment.

"It is fair to say that the United States has now joined most other countries in the world that have turned their faces against the juvenile death penalty," Mendoza wrote.

With the Mississippi Supreme Court decision being upheld today, 33 states reject the death penalty for juveniles.

Since 1995, there have been 23 such executions in the United States. The most recent was in 2004 in Texas. During that same time period, seven countries other than the United States have executed persons for crimes they committed as juveniles and all of the countries have subsequently disavowed the practice of executing juveniles.

Justice Elizabeth Washington filed a dissent from the new decision. Joined by Chief Justice Arnold Schwartz and Justice Clarice Murdock, Washington disputed the majority's points.

"Neither the meaning of our Eighth Amendment or the meaning of any of the other of our Constitution's amendments should be determined by the subjective views of the members of this court and like-minded foreigners," Washington wrote. "While personally I might support a minimum age of 18 for capital punishment, I cannot find a constitutional basis for doing so as a judge."

Mendoza's majority opinion was joined by Justices Randolph Smithson, Janice Beckman, Arlene Watson, Kenneth Warren and Doris Williams.

http://www.ussupremecourt.gov
http://www.deathtothedeathpenalty.com

News Story 6

Non-Stop World Flight Takes Off

SAN DIEGO—Millionaire adventurer Gary Harris took off this morning on his attempt to become the first person to complete a solo non-stop trip around the world in an airplane without refueling.

Harris, 63, the first person to complete an around-the-world trip in a hot-air balloon, took off from the San Diego Municipal Airport shortly before 6 a.m., PST, to begin his 62-hour, 23,000-mile journey.

"I'm a bit nervous," Harris said as he climbed into his E-Jett 555 jet plane. "I feel like a real test pilot. I'm confident things will go well, though. I've prepared well and I've got a great support crew."

The first around-the-world flight was completed by aviation pioneer Wiley Post in 1933. He stopped numerous times and took more than seven days to circumnavigate the globe. The first nonstop global flight without refueling by a duo was made in 1986 by Jeana Yeager and Dick Rutan.

Besides the non-stop record, Harris will be attempting to break several other aviation records, including the longest flight by a jet aircraft. That record of 12,000 miles was set in 1962 by a B-52 bomber.

The single-engine E-Jett 555 is carrying 18,100 pounds of fuel. Harris plans to fly at an average speed of 290 mph and rely on the jet stream to stretch his fuel. If all goes as planned, Harris should have about a 15% margin of extra fuel.

Harris will limit his diet to milkshakes.

"I'm sure I'll be too busy to worry about food too much," Harris said. "I'll be looking forward to a nice, juicy steak when I return, though."

http://garyharris.com

News Story 7

Non-Stop World Flight a Big Success

SAN DIEGO—Gary Harris has done it again. The millionaire adventurer has added another first to his credit. He became the first person to successfully circumnavigate the globe non-stop without refueling when he landed his E-Jett 555 aircraft at the San Diego Municipal Airport tonight at 8:18 p.m. PST.

Harris, 63, emerged from the cockpit, dressed in a golden flight suit, smiling and waving to the large crowd that had gathered to witness another first in aviation history.

"What a great day," he yelled to the crowd. "I'm so proud to become the first person to fly around the world non-stop. It's a milestone for pilots and airplane manufacturers."

Experts agreed with Harris.

"It's a monumental achievement in aviation," said Lawrence Finkle, the man who assesses scientific achievements for Guinness World Records. "It's on a par with the moon landing and the climbing of Mount Everest. It makes people sit up and take notice. And, more importantly, it inspires people, especially kids to dream about what can be accomplished."

The official time for the record-setting flight was 62 hours and 24 minutes. Harris had about 900 pounds of fuel left, enough to fly about another eight hours.

"I'm going to enjoy this for quite a while," Harris said, "but I'm not done chasing my dreams. I've got a few more things I want to do before I die."

http://www.garyharris.com

News Story 8

Man Without a Name Can Play the Guitar

LONDON—He was found on an island. He does not know who he is. He can play classical guitar like a master.

The morose-looking man was found three weeks ago on an island off the southeast coast of England. He was dripping wet and dressed in a tuxedo. He has spoken very few words and no one seems to know his name or nationality. He has spoken in English, French, Russian and German.

All anyone can say for sure is he can really play the guitar. According to medical personnel, the man usually plays classical pieces, but he has played a few folk songs and every so often he launches into a rock-and-roll song.

The mysterious case has caught the attention of the British public. Thousands of tips have been phoned in to the national missing persons hotline, but so far none has led anywhere.

Until he is positively identified, the "guitar guy," as he has come to be known, will remain in a mental hospital. Doctors say he is withdrawn, fearful and generally non-communicative. He often cringes when people approach him. Therapists speculate that he likely has suffered a severe emotional trauma.

"We're very concerned about him, Dr. Arlen Churchill said. "Most of the time, he just sits by himself. He stares straight ahead and rarely responds to any type of stimuli."

The "guitar guy," as British tabloids have dubbed the man, was found on the Isle of Sheppey, a quiet island and sailing resort near the mouth of the River Thames.

He is short, about 5-foot, 5-inches, and weighs 145 pounds. He has blonde hair and blue eyes. He has a small scar under his chin. Police officials estimate he is in his late 20s or early 30s.

About two weeks ago, caregivers gave the man a piece of paper and a pencil hoping that he might communicate with them more effectively by writing or drawing. Since he drew a crude picture of a man playing a guitar, the caregivers brought him a guitar. He's been playing it several hours a day ever since.

"He is much more calm and serene when he's playing the guitar," Dr. Churchill said. "He's like a different person. It gives us hope that soon he'll be able to tell us something about who he is and what happened to him."

http://www.namelessman.com

News Story 9

Obesity Linked to Income Levels

New obesity statistics are out.

Obesity is growing fastest among Americans who make more than $60,000 a year.

Study conducted by researchers at the University of Iowa. Results presented today at the annual conference of the American Heart Association in Las Vegas, Nevada.

Poor people are still the most likely to be overweight. The researchers say that people who have the lowest incomes a less likely to purchase expensive fresh produce and such products are often not readily available to them.

Quote from Dr. Mei Zhong, a professor in the School of Exercise and Nutritional Sciences at the University of Iowa:

> "There are way too many fast-food, high-fat options in low-income neighborhoods. When people don't have ready access to the proper foods, they, of course, turn to whatever substitutes are available to them. It's really no surprise that low-income Americans are more likely to be overweight than any other group."

Prof. Zhong and a team of graduate students examined stacks of documents and computer data from the National Health and Nutrition Examination Surveys. The research team found that last year, almost 30% of the people with incomes above $60,000 were obese. Twenty years ago, after accounting for inflation, just 9.7 percent of people with incomes above $60,000 were obese.

About 35% of people with incomes below $25,000 were obese. Twenty years ago, about 25% of poor people were obese.

Quote from Dr. Barbara Mueller, a professor in the Graduate School of Public Health at Midcity University:

> "Prof. Zhong's findings are interesting and important; however, I would caution against making any sweeping statements about social differences disappearing. Her study simply shows that obesity is affecting everybody. We still need to focus our attention on the main group of people who are most vulnerable. That's still clearly the poor. We have to find a way to get more and better information about nutrition and exercise to our poor. In addition, we have to find a way to ensure that our poor people have a chance to buy the foods necessary to live a healthier lifestyle and we have to find ways to make it possible for them and their children to exercise safely and effectively."

http://www.uiens.edu

News Story 10

Comatose Firefighter Wakes Up

Information from Midcity Fire Department:

Firefighter William Allen Loren, 43, who suffered brain damage more than 10 years ago when a burning beam fell on him while he was fighting a fire at a furniture warehouse and has since been virtually silent and almost completely blind, had a sudden and unexplained recovery this morning.

Loren began speaking to his wife during her regular daily visit and says he can see fine now.

Quote from Dr. Kent Davies, head physician, Monte Vista Convalescent Center:

"It's pretty much a miracle. When someone is virtually mute for more than a decade, you have to think he's not going to all of a sudden just regain his ability to speak. The return of his vision is another amazing development."

Since he began speaking, Loren has been surrounded by his wife, three children, other family members and former firefighter comrades.

Quote from Melinda Ann Loren, 40, Loren's wife:

"This is so wonderful. We've prayed for this for so long. We never gave up hope, but it's been really hard. He's such a wonderful man. I'm so glad he's back, but I feel sad that he's missed so much."

Pending medical tests, according to experts, the totality and likely duration of Loren's recovery are unknown. In similar cases, some patients have enjoyed total recovery, but others have relapsed within weeks or months.

In the fire at the McFadden Furniture Mart warehouse, Loren was knocked unconscious and suffered severe smoke inhalation. The severe head trauma and prolonged oxygen deprivation caused Loren to lapse into a coma that lasted for almost nine months.

Loren had received many citations for bravery during his nine-year career with the Midcity Fire Department. He was credited with saving the lives of seven people in a fire at an apartment complex in East Midcity about 12 years ago.

Loren's children: Riley Marie, 15; Matthew Mark; 13; Donna Allene; 11.

Quote from William Allen Loren:

"I can't believe I've been gone for more than 10 years. It seems like just yesterday when I ran into that burning warehouse. I've missed so much of my kids' lives. I just hope we can make up for lost time. I'm so grateful for all the support I've gotten. I know it probably sounds funny, but I feel like the luckiest man in the world right now."

Doctors plan to transfer Loren to Midcity General Hospital for a few days for testing and observation, but could release him to his family by next Monday.

http://www.mfd.gov

News Story 11

Laughing Good for What Ails You

Laughing could be good for you.

A new study has found that laughing causes the tissue that forms the inner lining of blood vessels, the endothelium, to expand and increase blood flow.

The same effect is caused by aerobic exercise.

Researchers from Midcity University presented their findings at the American College of Cardiology annual convention in Orlando, Florida, this afternoon.

The researchers asked 20 volunteers to watch a 15-minute segment of *Kingpin*, a 1996 comedy and then 48 hours later view the opening scenes from *Saving Private Ryan*, a 1998 war movie.

Researchers found that a stress-inducing movie can have negative effects on cardiac health, but a comedy can actually help improve cardiac health.

Quote from Dr. Gene Lamke, a professor in the Graduate School of Public Health at Midcity University and the lead author of the research paper:

> "It seems pretty clear that laughter induces the release of beneficial endorphins, just like exercise does. But we don't recommend that people replace exercise with simple laughing. A good, regular combination of the two is advisable, though."

Dr. Lamke and his team of researchers plan to conduct further research into the effects of laughter on cardiac health. He and his team have applied for state and federal grants to include more subjects in their studies and to study subjects over a period of years, not just days.

http://www.muschoolofpublichealth.edu

News Story 12

Poisonous Snack Kills 27 in the Philippines

MANILA, Philippines—Distraught parents, carrying the limp bodies of their children to hospitals, cursed, cried and wailed. A snack of cassava bought from an unknown vendor killed 27 and sickened 120 at an elementary school in the southern Philippines yesterday.

The roots of the cassava plant are rich in protein, minerals and the vitamins A, B and C. Cassava is often used as a snack; however, it can be poisonous if it is not thoroughly cooked and prepared properly. If it is eaten raw or prepared incorrectly, one of its chemical components interacts with digestive enzymes and the deadly poison cyanide is produced. Even small does of cassava can be fatal.

The victims suffered severe stomach pains, vomiting and diarrhea shortly after eating the morning snack. They were stricken at their school in Mabini, about 380 miles southeast of the capital, Manila.

A specimen of the deep-fried, caramelized cassava is being analyzed and authorities are searching for the vendor who sold the cassava to school cafeteria workers.

The woman who prepared the cassava was admitted to Garcia Memorial Provincial Hospital. She was suffering the same symptoms as the children. Authorities are hoping to talk with her as soon as possible to ascertain how the cassava was prepared.

Mabini Mayor Stephen Rances said 27 students were confirmed dead and at least 60 other children were in critical condition.

"The situation is extremely serious," Dr. Nenita Po said. "Cassava poisoning is tough to treat, but we're hopeful that we can save all the children who've made it to hospitals."

http://www.garciahospital.gov

News Story 13

Aspirin No Help in Women's Fight Against Heart Attacks

Gender differences are alive and well in medicine.

A major new study found that aspirin helps healthy women avoid strokes, but for most women, aspirin makes no difference in their risk of heart attacks.

The results are the total opposite of what has been found for men.

Aspirin is recommended for both men and women at high risk of heart disease.

Most doctors have assumed that since aspirin helped prevent heart problems in healthy men, it worked the same way for healthy women.

The new study raises issues associated with the dangers of generalization.

The findings were part of the Women's Health Study, a long-term, nationwide study funded by the National Heart, Lung and Blood Institute and the National Cancer Institute. A research team from Harvard University conducted the study.

Results were reported in the *New England Journal of Medicine* today.

The study was the first rigorous test of aspirin and vitamin E in women. It found that vitamin E did no good. A finding that is consistent with a large body of evidence.

Nearly 40,000 female health professionals 45 and older were randomly assigned to take either fake pills or 100 milligrams of aspirin every other day.

After 10 years, aspirin users had a 17% lower risk of stroke and a 24% lower risk for strokes caused by blood clots. Most strokes are caused by blood clots and aspirin is well-known for its anti-clotting properties, researchers said.

The results are generally good news, because women proportionately suffer more strokes and men suffer more heart attacks; therefore aspirin cuts the risk of the most pressing concern for each sex, researchers said. Reasons for the gender differences are unclear.

Last year, there were 345,000 heart attacks in U.S. women, and 373,000 strokes. Men suffered 520,000 heart attacks and 327,000 strokes.

The research team from Harvard University was headed by Dr. Kenneth Harres and Dr. Judy May.

"Our research shows that aspirin can certainly help improve cardiac health," Dr. May said, "but the best thing to do is to have a heart-healthy diet."

http://www.women'shealthstudy.com
http://www.ncs.org
http://www.nhlbi.org

News Story 14

Midcity University President Resigns

The President of Midcity University announced her resignation effective today.

Resignation turned in to Midcity University Board of Trustees.

Dr. Condoleesa Atwater cited the need for a fresh start for the university as the main reason for her resignation.

The Midcity University campus has been rocked in the past few months by a football recruiting scandal and reports that no male basketball player has actually graduated from the university in more than a decade.

Quote from Dr. Condolessa Atwater:

"It is clear to me that it is in the university's best interest that I remove the issue of my future from the debate so that nothing inhibits MU's ability to successfully create the bright future it so justly deserves. I am sorry that recent developments have cast a cloud of negativity over such a wonderful university. It has always been my intention to do whatever is necessary to help MU continue with its mission to be one of the top universities in the world."

The football recruiting scandal has been the most damaging issue. Media reports of allegations of rapes, strip club visits and sex parties for recruits have bombarded university officials for almost a year.

At least seven women have said they were assaulted by MU football players or recruits in the past four years.

An independent commission report released last month included findings that MU football coaches and players used sex, alcohol and marijuana as recruiting tools. The commission was appointed by the MU Board of Regents.

Just last week, a National Collegiate Athletic Association report examining graduation rates for college basketball programs, listed MU as the lowest rated Division I university. MU has not had a male basketball player obtain a degree in more than 10 years.

Quote from Sharon Penny, MU Board of Regents chairwoman:

"President Atwater will be missed, but the university has suffered greatly from a series of unfortunate controversies recently. Sadly, the problems appear to be growing rather than abating. Perhaps a fresh start with new leadership will bring the necessary perspectives required to turn things around."

Dr. Glen Broom, the vice-president for academic affairs at Midcity University, will serve as the interim president until a permanent replacement for Dr. Atwater can be selected.

A worldwide search for a new president could begin as early as next week, according to university sources who requested anonymity.

http://www.muadminstration.edu
http://www.paulanderson.com

News Story 15

Police Kill Man Who Rams Truck into County Jail

An odd incident at the Midcity County Jail this morning.

A man crashed a pickup truck into the side of the jail at 7:52 a.m.. He got out of the truck, ran inside the lobby of the jail, began yelling obscenities and brandishing a handgun.

He was fatally shot by Midcity police officers.

The man has been identified as Juan Jose Naranjo, 24, 1753 W. 95th Street.

He was airlifted to Midcity County Hospital with wounds to his torso, arms and legs. He was pronounced dead shortly after arrival.

At least 15 persons were in the lobby of the jail at the time of the incident, but no one else was hurt, according to homicide Lt. Ted McFadden.

Lt. McFadden was in the lobby of the jail at the time of the incident.

Quote from Lt. McFadden:

"We don't have a clue why the man rammed his truck into the side of the jail. If he was trying to break somebody out, he chose the wrong side of the jail. He smashed into the administration side. We're pretty sure it was an intentional act, but we haven't completely ruled out the possibility of a mechanical failure of some sort. Drugs or alcohol might be involved, too. He was really out of control when he entered the building."

Sheriff's officials locked down the jail for several hours after the incident.

A preliminary check of jail inmates found no relatives or suspected associates of Juan Jose Naranjo.

http://www.mpd.gov

News Story 16

Polio Found in Indonesia

The World Health Organization is reporting that a case of polio has been detected in Indonesia.

WHO officials report that the case is an indication that an outbreak spreading from northern Nigeria for more than two years has crossed an ocean and reached the world's fourth-most populous country.

WHO officials report that the virus was found in a village on the island of Java. The virus is most closely related to a strain of polio that was found in Saudi Arabia three months ago. Officials speculate that the virus was likely carried there either by an Indonesian who had worked in Saudi Arabia or by a pilgrim making a pilgrimage to Mecca.

Indonesia becomes the 16th country to be re-infected by a strain of the virus that broke out in northern Nigeria when vaccinations stopped there. It then crossed Africa and the Red Sea.

WHO officials are recommending that Indonesia immediately vaccinate five million children on the western end of Java, including the capital, Jakarta.

Indonesian government officials have indicated they are planning a large-scale inoculation program.

Each new case of polio diminishes the WHO's chances of reaching its goal of eradicating the disease by the end of the year.

The WHO has begun soliciting donors in an effort to increase efforts to contain the disease.

WHO officials report that genetic typing of the virus found in an 18-month-old boy in a village in West Java links it to the strain circulating in northern Nigeria and Saudi Arabia.

Dr. Nathan Freedman, chief of technical support in the WHO's polio division, examined the boy and talked with members of the boy's family.

Quote from Dr. Freedman:

> "None of the boy's family members had traveled to areas where polio is endemic, but other families in the boy's village had members who had been in Saudi Arabia as guest workers or pilgrims. It's pretty clear where the disease came from. We have several other cases in the same village that we're watching very closely. Clinically, they look a lot like polio."

http://www.who.org

News Story 17

Minimum Wage Hike Proposals Competing in U.S. Senate

WASHINGTON—Senate Republicans and Democrats are at it again. Competing proposals to raise the federal minimum wage are being debated and one or both of the proposals could be put to a vote later today.

The Democratic plan would increase the current $5.15 hourly minimum by more than $2. The increase would take effect over 26 months and be phased-in via three installments. The GOP proposal would be another phased-in program, raising the minimum wage by $1.10 in two increments of 55 cents each over 18 months.

It is not clear if either proposal has enough support to pass. A compromise bill is likely, according to Senate watchers.

Even if a bill is passed out of the Senate, a minimum wage increase faces a much tougher road in the more conservative House.

According to House Majority Leader Caitlin McFadden, R-Washington, there are no plans to vote this year on a minimum wage increase.

"Most business groups, especially small-businessmen, don't want an increase," Rep. McFadden said. "They tell me that a hike in the minimum wage will drive up costs and force them to lay off workers. No one wants that."

The federal minimum wage was $2.65 in 1978. In 1991, it was raised to $4.25. In 1997, it was increased to $5.15.

http://www.ussenatedemocrats.gov
http://www.ussenaterepublicans.gov

News Story 18

Minimum Wage Hike Bills Fail

WASHINGTON—Dueling proposals to raise the $5.15 federal minimum wage were defeated in the Senate today. Both plans fell well short of the number of votes needed for passage.

"It's a disgrace that someone who works 40 hours a week, 52 weeks a year has to live in poverty in the richest country in the world," said Sen. Karen Murphy, D-Mass., who argued in favor of the Democratic proposal to increase the minimum wage by $2.10 over the next 26 months.

The Republican proposal featured a smaller increase—$1.10 over 18 months. Supporters said the smaller increase would help workers without hurting employers.

"Workers just entering the job market and those without many marketable skills deserve to make more money, but we have to keep small business owners in mind, too," said Kent Davies, R-Wyo., who pushed hard for the Republican proposal.

"We knew it was going to be tough to get either proposal approved, but now that the issue has been debated fully and the media have covered the issue reasonably well, we hope that many of the state minimum-wage initiatives will have a greater chance of being successful," said Sylvia Ramsden, D-CA.

More than 30 states will vote on proposed increases to the minimum wage in the next year.

"We're not going to give up on increasing the federal minimum wage," said Sharon Ishida, D-Hawaii. "It's too important an issue to just give up. One good thing that came from the debate this time was the clear difference between the Democratic and Republican proposals. People need to know which party is working harder for more Americans."

http://www.ussenatedemocrats.gov
http://www.ussenaterepublicans.gov

News Story 19

Wayward Wheel Whacks Local Cop

A wheel flew off a car and struck a Midcity Police Department officer, breaking his leg, as he stood on the shoulder of Interstate 30 writing a traffic ticket this morning.

The accident occurred about 7 a.m. in the westbound lanes just west of Burris Drive.

Authorities closed the two right-side freeway lanes for about a mile, forcing commuters to a 15-mph crawl in the remaining two lanes. Congestion cleared after about an hour.

The officer, Jerald P. Kerry, 37, was transported by ambulance to Midcity General Hospital, according to David Cohen, MPD spokesperson.

Quote from David Cohen, MPD Public Information Officer:

"Officer Kerry had pulled over a motorist for excessive speed. He parked his motorcycle behind the car of the suspect vehicle. As he was writing out the ticket, a tow truck passed by and a wheel from the car being towed flew off. It ricocheted off the car of the driver being ticketed and slammed into Officer Kerry's left leg. Officer Kerry radioed for help and within minutes help arrived."

Kerry is listed in satisfactory condition, according to doctors at Midcity General Hospital.

The tow truck driver, David Muller, 52, saw what happened and pulled off the freeway and returned to the scene to provide assistance. Muller is cooperating with the investigation, according to Cohen.

http://www.mpd.gov

News Story 20

Midcity Roads Ranked Sixth Worst in U.S.

Midcity's freeways and roads rated sixth worst in the nation among major urban populations.

The Road Information Program, known as TRIP, released its annual report this morning. The industry group studies wear and tear on roads as part of its efforts to lobby for increased state and federal funding for roads, streets and highways.

The TRIP report reported 58% of Midcity's interstates, highways and major roads have pavement in poor condition.

Last year, TRIP reported that 60% of Midcity's interstates, highways and major roads had pavement in poor condition. Last year, Midcity was rated the fourth worst city in the nation for the quality of its streets and freeways.

Nationwide, TRIP reports that 26% of major metropolitan roads are substandard.

Quote from Ronald Moore, mayor of Midcity:

"We're not happy with the results, of course, but at least we're making some progress at addressing the problems with our roads. It's going to take at least a couple more years before we see any significant improvement in the quality of our roads. We just don't have the money to do the large-scale repairs and resurfacing that's needed, but we're hopeful and the state and federal government will come through with some emergency funding in the next six months."

TRIP is a Washington, D.C, non-profit group backed by highway engineering and construction businesses, labor unions and other groups that support increased road-building and repair. The TRIP report is based on an annual Federal Highway Administration survey of pavement conditions.

Rankings (percentages of pavement deemed "unacceptable" in parentheses):

Kansas City, Mo. (71%)	Midcity (58%)
San Jose, CA. (67%)	New Orleans, LA. (55%)
St. Louis, Mo. (66%)	Boston, MA. (49%)
Los Angeles, CA. (64%)	Sacramento, CA. (49%)
San Francisco/Oakland, CA. (60%)	Oklahoma City, OK. (47%)

TRIP ranked California as the worst overall state for road conditions.

TRIP indicated that in addition to the 58% of Midcity's roads that were judged "unacceptable," 28% of Midcity roads were judged "mediocre."

TRIP reported that Midcity's poor roads cost the average motorist $625 a year in higher operating costs, well above the national average of $401. The higher costs are related to faster vehicle deterioration, increased maintenance, tire wear and higher fuel consumption.

TRIP found only three urban areas with populations of more than 500,000 where at least 75% of the roads were in good condition: Atlanta, GA., Orlando, FL., and Phoenix, AZ.

Quote from Wilma G. Watkins, executive director of TRIP:

"Our report should be seen as a wake-up call for Congress, state and local governments. Congress especially should help state and local transportation officials by approving long-term highway funding bills."

http://www.tripresearch.org

News Story 21

General Motors and Toyota Have Best Cars

DETROIT—In 15 of 18 categories in a survey of new car models, General Motors Corp. and Toyota Motor Co., the world's two largest automakers, had the top vehicles, according to research firm J.D. Power and Associates.

The Lexus SC430 from Toyota was the highest-ranking vehicle for the second year in a row. Owners of the luxury coupe reported 54 problems per 100 vehicles. Suzuki Motor Corp. had the highest number of problems—151 per 100 vehicles. The industry average was 118 problems per 100 vehicles.

Toyota had the top vehicles in 10 categories. Among Toyota's winners were the hybrid Prius in the compact car category, the Sienna in the minivan category and Lexus sedans swept the three luxury car categories.

GM had five winners. The GM winners included the Buick LeSabre in the full-size car category; the Chevy Suburban in the full-size sport utility vehicle category; and the GMC Sierra in the heavy-duty, full-size pickup truck category.

The top-ranking foreign brand was Jaguar with 88 problems per 100 vehicles.

The J.D. Power and Associates survey is the 19th annual. Researchers interviewed 62,300 people within 90 days of buying or leasing a new vehicle this year. The survey includes 135 variables associated with a new vehicle including braking, handling, engine troubles, seat comfort and sound systems.

http://www.jdpower&associates.com

News Story 22

Eiffel Tower Fire Handled Quickly

PARIS—An electrical fire within the Eiffel Tower startled tourists and alarmed people all across the city this morning. The fire was extinguished quickly and the fire was contained to a small portion of the top corner of the Eiffel Tower.

The sight of the city's best-known landmark with smoke rising far into the morning sky was unsettling to tourists and residents alike since several threats to the tower had been issued in the past couple of months by various terrorists groups.

"I was sure a plane or something had flown into the tower," said Michelle M. Medina, 26, a tourist from New Jersey. "I thought we were having another 9-11."

About 10 years ago, French commandos spoiled a plot by Algerian hijackers to fly a plane into the Eiffel Tower.

"The fire was caused by a faulty electrical wire in the standard equipment room," said Commandant Christian Decolloredo, a spokesperson for the Paris Fire Department.

The fire began about 9:15 a.m. in an area that is closed to tourists. Flames quickly spread and witnesses on the ground reported seeing flames in the tower. About 2,500 visitors had to be evacuated down the 1,070-foot tower's winding stairs.

About 125 firefighters and 20 fire trucks responded to the emergency call. The fire was extinguished in about one hour. The tower was closed for about three hours, but was reopened in the early afternoon. The elevator will be closed for several days, though as a security precaution, according to tower officials.

Fires have hit the Eiffel Tower before. In 2000, a safety net caught fire. A kitchen fire in a lower-level kitchen occurred in 1998. In 1956, a fire in a television transmitter raged through the top of the tower.

The tower, which opened in 1889, draws about 6 million visitors per year.

"I was pretty disappointed," said Cole T. Kegel, 22, of Los Angeles, Calif. "I waited in line a long time to buy a ticket to ride the elevator to the top and I wasn't allowed to take my ride. I didn't get my money back, either. I'm bummed. It's only about five bucks, but I might not ever get back here to do it."

There were no injuries and no damage estimate has been issued so far.

http://www.eiffeltowerinfo.com

News Story 23

News Release **News Release** **News Release** **News Release** **News Release**

News from Midcity University

Contact Laurie Lynne
1.877.555-MUMU

For Immediate Release

According to a research team at Midcity University, the color of an athlete's uniform can make a difference when it comes to athletic success or failure.

Researchers in the School of Exercise and Nutritional Sciences at Midcity University have recently completed an examination of four sports in the latest summer Olympic Games to determine if uniform color has any relationship to winning or losing. Their findings were that competitors who wore red uniforms were more likely to win their competitions.

"In all the sports we studied, we find that wearing red is consistently associated with a much higher probability of winning," said Dr. Melissa J. Wulf, a professor and senior researcher, School of Exercise and Nutritional Sciences, Midcity University. "It was a bit surprising, but the numbers don't lie. The differences are too great statistically to be just a coincidence."

Red coloration is often associated with aggression in animals and usually dominant males have scarlet markings, according to Dr. Wulf. In addition, wearing red might deliver implicit messages of vigor and danger, she said.

"The effect of the color red may subconsciously intimidate opponents in sports," Dr. Wulf suggested. "The effect may be most pronounced when athletes are relatively equal in skill and strength."

In their study, the Midcity University researchers analyzed the results in four contact sports at the summer games: boxing, tae kwon do, Greco-Roman wrestling and freestyle wrestling. In the selected events, participants were randomly assigned red protective gear and other sportswear.

Athletes wearing red gear or uniforms won more often in 16 of 21 rounds of competition.

"Wearing red does not guarantee a victory, " said Dr. Wulf. "Our research was confined to evenly matched competitors. If your opponent is much bigger and better than you are, wearing red isn't going to turn you into Superman or some other invincible super hero or super athlete."

The colors of Midcity University sports teams are black and gold.

Professor Melissa Wulf can be reached at mwulf@mu.edu.

More information available at http://www.muens.edu

News Story 24

Police Fatally Shoot Sword-Swinging Killer at Supermarket

Midcity police officers shot and killed a man early this afternoon at a West Midcity Food Basket supermarket. The man was brandishing a samurai-style sword and had killed three people and injured four others.

Two of the deceased victims were shoppers and one was a Food Basket employee. Two of the wounded were store employees and two were shoppers.

Witnesses reported that shortly after 1 p.m., a man wearing a Hawaiian-print bathing suit and a black tank top entered the supermarket carrying a long, slender cardboard box. Once inside the store, he slid a samurai-style sword out of the box. He started yelling obscenities, ran to the back of the store and started assaulting people.

The three people were dead with police officers arrived. They confronted the man, but he refused to drop his sword. When he advanced toward four officers, they opened fire. He died at the scene.

The injured people were taken to Midcity Memorial Hospital. Doctors report that all are in "satisfactory" condition with lacerations and contusions.

Alleged killer identified as Aaron Peter Simpson, 31, 4971 Summerdale Place, West Midcity.

Deceased people:

    Alicia Lucinda Gonzales, 29, 8726 Talon Dr., West Midcity (shopper)
    Jeffrey Allen Norton, 42, 9111 Crest St., West Midcity (shopper)
    Terry Martin McGinley, 51, 721 Martin Ct., North Midcity (employee)

Injured people:

    Monica Maureen Monet, 38, 8863 W. 97th St., West Midcity (shopper)
    Lindsay Lynn Maxwell, 19, 3855 Highdale Rd., West Midcity (shopper)
    Alexander Paul Mascari, 55, 1830 Mast Blvd., West Midcity (employee)
    Carolyn Patricia Appleton, 46, 6226 Nottingham Way, West Midcity (employee)

Quote from David Cohen, public information officer, Midcity Police Department:

"We don't have a motive for the attack right now. Mr. Simpson was not an ex-employee, but several employees remember seeing him in the store before. It could be that he just snapped. He lived very close to the store and probably just wanted to be somewhere he was familiar with. Our officers gave him every opportunity to surrender peacefully, but he chose to advance toward them with the sword still in his hands. The officers had no choice but to fire at him."

All information provided by David Cohen, Midcity Police Department Public Information Officer.

http://www.mpd.gov

News Story 25

12 Die in Chicago Party Disaster

CHICAGO—A dozen people died and at least four dozen others were injured seriously when a third-floor deck collapsed during a party early this morning. When the floor collapsed, wood and bodies were sent crashing to the ground. The weight of the third floor smashing into the second floor sent the second floor crashing to the ground as well.

Most of the people who died were crushed by the weight of the third and second floors collapsing. The accident occurred about 1:45 a.m.

"There were people covering me. It was pitch black and people were yelling. It all happened so fast. I thought I was going to die," said Nancy Ellen Gompers, 21, who suffered injuries to her hip and shoulder.

Witnesses said at least 50 people had jammed their way onto the third floor deck of an apartment for the party in the city's affluent Lincoln Park neighborhood.

"The music was loud and people were talking, but I heard a sort or rumbling sound and then a big cracking noise and then the floor just gave way," said Gary B. Foster, 23, who suffered a broken leg and numerous lacerations, contusions and abrasions.

Seven women and five men, most of them reportedly partying on the second deck and first-floor patio below the third-floor deck were apparently sandwiched between the falling floors, were killed, according to Jerald T. Jackson, a spokesman for the city's Office of Emergency Management.

Nine people were pronounced dead at the scene, and the Cook County Medical Examiner's office confirmed that three other people were dead on arrival at a hospital. Many of the injured people are reportedly in critical condition so the death toll could increase significantly.

"Apparently, the party was a birthday celebration that had been widely publicized, so the crowd was much bigger than the organizers had anticipated," Jackson said. "There obviously was just too much weight and pressure on that upper deck. It looks as if it just gave way and once it went, the whole thing collapsed. The people below didn't really have much of a chance."

http://www.chicagopd.gov

News Story 26

Killer Thunderstorms Slash Through Midwest and East

MEMPHIS, Tenn.—A line of deadly thunderstorms swept through the Ohio Valley toward the East Coast yesterday. Five people, including three Ohioans and two Tennesseans were killed and at least 15 other people were injured by the storms.

The storms spawned at least two tornadoes, one in Ohio and one in New York. The tornado in Ohio damaged about 100 homes in Youngstown. The tornado in upstate New York damaged about 25 homes near Catskill.

The deceased in Ohio included a 12-year-old boy who drowned in a rain-swollen ditch, a 19-year-old man who was struck by lightening, and a 52-year-old woman who drowned in an apartment complex laundry room when she was trapped by rising waters.

The deceased in Tennessee included a 68-year-old man who was crushed to death when a tree fell on his home and a 15-year-old girl who drowned while trying to save her 8-year-brother from a raging drainage culvert. The boy was rescued by emergency workers.

The storm, with winds whipping up to 60 mph, felled trees throughout the Memphis area, trapping hundreds of people in their businesses, vehicles and homes. Power outages shut down Memphis International Airport for several hours.

In Catskill, the winds tore roofs off of homes and businesses and overturned cars and trucks.

In Illinois, about 160,000 customers lost electrical power overnight as violent thunderstorms with winds up to 100 mph ripped across the northern two-thirds of the state.

Mayors of several cities and governors of several states are expected to declare states of emergency as a result to the devastating thunderstorms.

http://www.nationalweatherservice.gov

News Story 27

Mayor's Budget Plan Cuts Jobs and Programs

Midcity Mayor Ronald Moore unveiled his proposed budget for next year this morning.

The proposed budget cuts 360 jobs, calls for the closing of all community service centers, limits library hours significantly and eliminates portions of a popular child-care program. The layoffs and other money-saving moves are designed to save about $51.5 million.

Moore is recommending that public safety be funded at slightly higher levels, despite the dire revenue projections for next year. His proposal calls for the police and fire budgets to be increased by a combined total of $34.3 million.

Most city departments will have to absorb cuts under the proposed $857.7 million general fund budget. The general fund pays for such day-to-day functions as police and fire protection, street maintenance and park and recreation activities.

The city has kept many jobs vacant this year, but even so, the proposed budget necessitates the laying off of about 290 of the city's 11,000 workers. About 33% of those targeted for layoff are managers. Moore says letting those supervisors go would save the city about $1.9 million.

Quote from Mayor Moore:

"I don't like having to take people's jobs away. I feel very bad for those people who are going to lose their jobs. They've been doing a good job, serving the city well. It's just that we are in such dire straits, we have to take drastic actions to get the city back on solid economic footing."

The cuts aimed at community services, parks, libraries and child care would save almost $10.5 million.

No immediate reaction from the Board of Supervisors. The Board of Supervisors will begin holding hearings on the mayor's budget proposals next week. A majority of the Board must approve the mayor's budget before it can be implemented. In the past, the Board often has asked the mayor to revise his budget proposals.

Employee costs account for nearly 80% of the city's budget.

Specifics of Moore's proposal include the following:

1. Cut $3.8 million from the Community and Economic Development Department budget. This would include $2.6 million from the "6-to-6" child care program which is offered free at 178 local elementary and middle schools. In addition, all of the city's community services centers would close and homeless programs would be significantly reduced.

2. Cut $3.5 million from the Parks and Recreation Department budget, plus eliminate 65 jobs. Reduce recreation center hours from 48 per week to 40 per week.

3. Cut $2.9 million from libraries, plus eliminate 21 jobs. Reduce hours to a maximum of 44 per week.

http://www.midcitymayor.gov
http://www.midcitymuniemployees.org

News Story 28

Airport Screeners' Evaluation and Training Rated Poor

WASHINGTON—The Transportation Security Administration has failed to establish a standard to measure the quality of its airport screeners and has not provided adequate training for the screeners, according to a congressional report released this morning.

The Government Accounting Office report is critical of the ability of TSA screeners to detect guns, weapons and other dangerous items and faults the TSA for failing to set a standard for the screeners so it can develop ways and means to improve the performance of the screeners.

"Weaknesses and vulnerabilities continue to exist in passenger and checked baggage screening systems at airports of all sizes, at airports with federal screeners and at airports with private-sector screeners," the report said.

The GAO report urged the TSA to develop standards for how many "threat objects" a screener finds when undercover agents try to slip such objects through at checkpoints.

"Without performance targets for covert testing, TSA will not have identified a desired level of performance related to screener detection of threat objects," the report said.

TSA officials, responding to the GAO report, said they have created broad performance guidelines for screeners that include periodic testing and goals related to the number of passengers that should be screened during a specified period of time. The TSA indicated that individual performance standards should be available within six months.

Current laws require that screeners receive 40 hours of classroom instruction and 60 hours of on-the-job training before they are permitted to check passengers or luggage. TSA policy requires that screeners also receive an average of three hours of refresher training per week.

http://www.tsa.gov
http://www.gao.gov

Story 29

Australian Woman Sentenced to 20 Years for Pot Smuggling

BALI, Indonesia—A woman from Australia was convicted of smuggling 8 pounds of marijuana onto Bali island and was sentenced to 20 years in prison today.

Darlene Elaine Allenby, 26, wept when the verdict was announced. Her case has attracted worldwide media attention, but interest was especially high in her native Australia.

Allenby was arrested six months ago when airport authorities discovered bundles of marijuana in her surfboard traveling bag when she arrived on Bali with her family for a vacation. Her lawyers argued that the marijuana was planted in her bag by airport handlers in Australia. Several airport workers in Australia have been arrested in the past few months on suspicion of drug smuggling.

Public opinion polls in Australia during the past two months consistently have shown that the majority of Australians believe Allenby's claims that the marijuana was planted in her surfboard bag.

Allenby faced the possibility of the death penalty, but prosecutors requested a life sentence instead. Judge Wayan Suastrawan meted out a sentence of 20 years, because Allenby has never been in legal trouble before.

The Australian government has offered to send senior lawyers to Bali to help Allenby and her attorneys with her appeal. In addition, Australian government officials have offered to permit Allenby to serve her sentence in Australia.

"I don't know if Ms. Allenby is guilty or innocent," Australian Prime Minister Tony Rimmer said. "But I would ask that we all refrain from rushing to judgment and remember that we need to respect the culture and practices of the countries we choose to visit and we must be aware that when we leave home, we are subject to the laws, rules, regulations and customs of the countries we visit."

Customs officials in Bali testified that when Allenby was asked to open her surfboard bag, she looked "nervous" and made efforts to avoid opening the bag.

On the witness stand, Allenby testified that she was reluctant to open the bag, because the zipper was faulty and she had packed all of her toiletries in the bag. She feared she would not be able to repack everything and close the bag in time to catch the shuttle to her hotel.

http://www.balicourts.gov
http://www.australiapm.gov

News Story 30

Drug Store Employee Fatally Shoots Woman

Most of the information provided by Dave Cohen, public information officer, Midcity Police Department.

An employee at a North Midcity Buy-Rite drug store says he shot and killed a woman who tried to rob the store last night, because the woman threatened him with a weapon.

The attempted robbery of the Buy-Rite on Aspen Ave. near Pine St. was reported to police at 10:53 p.m.

Patrol officers arrived at the drug store about six minutes later and found the body of Christina Arlene Yamaguchi, 33, 2093 Mercer Dr., North Midcity, near the cash register by the front entrance.

The weapon that Yamaguchi allegedly tried to grab just before she was shot to death was still tucked in the waistband of her jeans. Police officers have determined that the weapon was a plastic replica of a revolver.

The employee who shot Yamaguchi, Victor K. Rusk, 41, told police he thought the woman seemed suspicious when she walked into the store. She reportedly shopped for a few minutes then came to the cash register and demanded money.

Rusk has worked for Buy-Rite for 15 years. He's been an assistant manager at the Aspen Ave. store for 7 years.

Quote from Victor Rusk:

"I shot the woman when she reached for her gun. She had a weird look on her face. I was scared. I really thought my life was in jeopardy. We've been robbed so many times this year. I didn't want to shoot, but to me, it came down to her or me."

There were two other Buy-Rite employees in the store at the time of the shooting. Both confirmed Rusk's version of the events.

Yamaguchi was found wearing dark clothing, a black watch cap and latex gloves.

The police investigation into the incident is continuing.

Quote from Dave Cohen, MPD public information officer:

"An employee of a business has the right to shoot someone if he or she feels his or her life is being threatened. Employees, like regular citizens, are allowed to defend themselves and to use deadly force in life-threatening situations."

http://www.mpd.gov

News Story 31

Love-Sick Woodpecker Ticks Off South Midcity Residents

MIDCITY—Many car and truck owners in South Midcity are covering their mirrors in an effort to put one over on an amorous woodpecker. The bird apparently thinks that when he sees his reflection in a mirror, he's seeing a rival.

Tom Jensen, who owns Discount Auto Glass, said he has replaced at least 50 smashed mirrors so far this year because of the woodpecker. Apparently, the bird has staked out the Rancho Midcity area of South Midcity as his territory.

"People are getting pretty mad about it," Jensen said. "One guy's been in my shop four times in the past couple of months. He says he keeps forgetting to cover up his mirrors."

Local birdwatcher, Stanley Jamison, is not surprised by the single-minded bird.

"During breeding season especially, male woodpeckers aggressively defend their turf," Jamison said. "It really doesn't matter if the perceived threat is a real bird or a reflection in a mirror. If a woodpecker thinks he's got a rival, he's going to fight."

Courtney Moore has had two mirrors on her Chrysler Sebring smashed. She witnessed the bird attacking a neighbor's car.

"I yelled at the bird and he quit pecking at the driver's side mirror," she said. "But then, he just walked across the front windshield and pecked on the passenger side mirror. I was dumbfounded."

Local animal control officers said they have no plans to try to capture or kill the offending woodpecker.

"All people have to do is drape a towel or rag over their mirrors," Jamison said. "The woodpecker will eventually find a mate and then he'll be too busy to worry about attacking his reflection in the mirrors."

http://www.midcitybirdlovers.org

News Story 32

Bombs Kill 25 in Indonesia

JAKARTA, Indonesia—Two bomb blasts today in a busy market in central Indonesia killed at least 25 people and wounded more than 50 people, police reported.

The early-morning explosions happened in the Christian-dominated town of Tentena, according to police. The region has been a hotbed for violence between Muslims and Christians for more than a decade.

According to witnesses, the first explosion was a small one and caused only minor damage and injuries, but about 10 minutes after the first explosion, another more powerful explosion flattened a produce market and claimed most of the casualties.

Indonesia is the world's most populous Muslim nation, but Poso, the area that includes the blast zone, has roughly equal numbers of Muslims and Christians. About three years ago, about 1,000 people died in fighting between Muslims and Christians in Poso, which is about 35 miles from Tentena and about 1,000 miles northeast of Jakarta.

Two days ago, tips about possible attacks from an anonymous source to officials at the United States embassy, led to the temporary closure of the embassy and other diplomatic offices in Indonesia. According to sources, the embassy and other diplomatic offices will remain closed until further notice.

http://www.indonesianews.com

News Story 33

Latest Rock-Throwing Results in Death

Most of the information obtained from Lt. David Garcia, Midcity Police Department.

Another rock attack this morning. One person died as a result of the incident.

This is the fifth consecutive day that rock-throwing has been reported in the East Midcity area.

At about 8:30 this morning, 24-year-old Hilary M. Park, 7621 Daisy Ct., East Midcity, was killed when a soft-ball-sized rock smashed through her vehicle's windshield.

The attack on Park was one of four separate rock-throwing incidents that have been reported today so far.

In all, over the past five days, 18 rock-throwing incidents have been reported in the East Midcity area.

Most of the rocks have been thrown from fast-moving vehicles, but some have been launched from overpasses.

Park died shortly after being hit in the head when she and her husband were returning home after dropping off their daughter at school.

Quote from Raymond H. Park, husband of Hilary Park:

"We were just driving along and talking. A car whizzed by us and our windshield exploded. I looked at my wife and there was blood all over her."

Park stopped the car and called police. Paramedics arrived within three minutes, but they were unable to save Mrs. Park.

Police are asking that anyone with information about any of the rock-throwing incidents, but particularly the one that resulted in Park's death, to call them.

Numbers to call:

555.555.9191
555.555.TIPS

Quote from Lt. Garcia:

"These attacks seem to be random, but they're definitely intentional. We don't think the incidents are simple pranks. Some one or several some ones seem to want to do harm to people and property."

Many of the rocks, including the five-pounder that killed Park, are being examined for fingerprints and other forensic evidence.

So far, witnesses have reported seeing people in cars and trucks throwing rocks at passing vehicles.

Police say there is little motorists can do to protect themselves from these kinds of attacks.

Quote from Jennifer Armstrong, assistant chief, Midcity Police Department:

"The people responsible for these attacks will be brought to justice. We have teams of investigators devoting full-time to finding the cowards who are preying on innocent, unsuspecting citizens."

http://www.mpd.gov

News Story 34

Committee Formed to Save "6-to-6" Program

The Midcity Unified School District has formed a committee to explore ways to save a popular before- and after-school program that is slated to be significantly cut, actually eliminated, at at least 25 schools.

The committee is composed of retired teachers, retired school administrators, marketing experts and established fund-raisers.

The $2.6 million cut in the "6-to-6" program is part of Mayor Ronald Moore's budget proposal for next year.

The 6-to-6 program currently serves more than 22,000 students at 178 elementary and middle schools free of charge.

The program gets the bulk of its funding from state and federal grants.

The cutback could mean that about 2,200 students would not be able to participate in the 6-to-6 program next year.

The 6-to-6 program provides homework assistance, arts, crafts, sports and other supervised activities for children before and after school.

The 6-to-6 program opens at 6 a.m. and closes at 6 p.m. It does not operate during the traditional school day—8:00-2:00—except to accept kindergarten students at 12:30.

One option being explored to keep all of the 6-to-6 programs operating is to start charging parents small fees for each child enrolled.

Quote from Dr. Sonja Benjamin, deputy superintendent, Midcity Unified School District:

"We're going to do everything possible to keep the program going at all the schools in the district. We're talking to a lot of the local businesses and associations about donating money, supplies and even personnel. And, if we have to, we'll institute a reasonable fee structure for those parents who can pay for the service."

Last year, the 6-to-6 program had a budget of $25.3 million.

http://www.musd.edu
http://www.6-to-6.program.org

News Story 35

Midcity University Gets $4 Million Donation

A Midcity man has donated $4 million to Midcity University.

Franklin P. Brown, 79, wants his money to be used for scientific research at his alma mater.

The donation is not a record-breaking gift, but what is interesting about the gift is it is not from an institute, corporation, foundation or part of an estate. It is a gift from a guy named Frank who made a lot of money and wants to give some of it back to help others.

Quote from Franklin Brown:

"I hope my gift can make a difference for young scholars who want to do serious research. Midcity University was good to me all those years ago and now it's my turn to do something nice for the university."

Brown was a chemistry major at Midcity University. He used his degree in connection with careers in the soft drink industry, the oil industry and the candy industry.

Brown never married and has no brothers or sisters.

Quote from Dr. Sheila Jefferson, dean, College of Sciences, Midcity University:

"This is a wonderfully generous gift from Mr. Brown. The money will go a long way toward helping educate and train young scientists who will be leaders in their fields in the years to come. We plan to use about half of the money for scholarships and the rest to create the 'Franklin P. Brown Research Laboratory.'"

The scholarship program will be called the Franklin P. Brown Scholarship. The money will come from an endowment established with half of Brown's donation. The first scholarships, at least three each year, will be awarded for the next academic year.

Ground will be broken for the Franklin P. Brown Research Laboratory at the end of next month, according to Dr. Jefferson. Plans for the lab were developed last semester, when Mr. Brown announced that he was planning to make his donation.

http://www.mufoundation.edu
http://www.franklinbrown.com

News Story 36

MU Lab Used to Create Illegal Drugs

A Midcity University laboratory was used by a graduate student to make methamphetamine, Ecstasy and fentanyl, an anesthetic eighty times more potent than morphine, according to Midcity police officials.

Midcity police arrested MU graduate student, Philip N. Van Zant, 26, 8632-B Emerald Court, this morning at his apartment.

The MU campus laboratory where Van Zant worked has been shut down. University officials have indicated that the lab should be reopened by Monday of next week.

Investigators from the Drug Enforcement Administration are conducting an investigation into the allegations.

Quote from Kevin Davis, DEA spokesman:

> "We seized capsules of Ecstasy, vials of fentanyl and some marijuana plants from Mr. Van Zant's apartment. In addition, Mr. Van Zant has admitted using the campus lab to manufacture methamphetamine, Ecstasy and fentanyl."

Van Zant, who is pursuing a master's degree in chemistry, is on probation for drug violations three years ago. He was convicted of growing marijuana and manufacturing Ecstasy.

Quote from Dr. Sheila Jefferson, dean, College of Sciences, Midcity University:

> "We've had students arrested before for drug violations, but I can't recall another time when university facilities were used in the manufacture of illegal substances. We monitor our labs very closely, but Mr. Van Zant managed to beat our system for a while. The fact that he endangered others, including many of his fellow students, with his illegal activity is especially troubling. I'm glad we've put an end to the very inappropriate and dangerous misuse of our labs."

According to the DEA, a hidden surveillance camera in the lab caught Van Zant working with a dark liquid that later tested positive for Ecstasy. The DEA and MU officials had been tipped last week that illegal activity was taking place in the science labs, so surveillance cameras were installed.

According the MU officials, there are strict controls on its laboratories, which do some of the more and $200,000,000 worth of research the university performs each year.

Van Zant is scheduled to appear in court tomorrow.

http://www.mupublicsafety.edu
http://www.mpd.gov
http://www.dea.gov

News Story 37

Prank Fails to Amuse and Costs Local Boys $900

Two teenage boys have been ordered to pay $900 in medical bills for a woman who says she was so startled by a prank the boys played that she had to visit a hospital.

Thomas C. Macmillan, 17, and Gregory A. Zimmer, 16, placed a talking stuffed toy bear on the porch of Margaret Anne Ostergard, 68, one night three months ago. They knocked on her door and then hid in the bushes to watch her reaction when she came to the door and saw the talking bear.

Quote from Margaret Ostergard:

"I saw some shadowy figures outside my house and then heard some loud banging on my front door. I called out and asked, 'Who's there?' but no one answered. I was frightened. I didn't know what to think. I hid in the bathroom at the back of the house all night."

The next morning, Mrs. Ostergard reported that she was still shaking and had an upset stomach, so she went to the emergency room at Midcity General Hospital.

The teenagers' families had offered to pay Mrs. Ostergard's medical expenses, but she declined and sued. She said she did not believe the boys were sincere in their apologies since they were not offered in person, but were presented to her by attorneys for the two families.

Judge Milton W. Perkins declined to award Mrs. Ostergard punitive damages. He said he did not believe the boys acted maliciously, but he did award Mrs. Ostergard enough money to pay all her hospital expenses.

Quote from Sean C. Macmillan, 44, father of Thomas Macmillan:

"We're glad to have this unfortunate incident behind us. The boys realize that what they thought was a practical joke on a neighbor was not really funny at all. They're sincerely sorry for what they did. They're good kids. Good students. I'm sure they've learned a valuable lesson. We're happy Mrs. Ostergard is feeling better now, too."

http://www.midcitycourts.gov

News Story 38

Woman Dies in Fiery Crash on Route 56

A motorist died last night after a collision on Route 56 sent her pickup plunging off a ramp 50 feet to the ground where it caught fire, according to Midcity police officials.

Many motorists stopped to help or watch. Several blasted the flames with fire extinguishers and water from a nearby creek. Their efforts failed to save the life of Yolanda M. Greene, 34, 613 Hill St.

The crash occurred on the on-ramp from Hill Street to Route 56 at 11:52 p.m. last night, according to Midcity police officials. Greene's pickup collided with another pickup where the ramp narrows from two lanes to one. The pickup driven by Joshua S. Teaby, 19, 5328 Pearson Dr., veered left and rolled over. Greene's vehicle veered right and its momentum carried it over the guide rail. It fell about 50 feet and burst into flames.

Greene was found dead in the burned wreckage of her Toyota pickup truck. Teaby's Ford pickup truck sustained major damage.

All information obtained from David Cohen, public information officer, Midcity Police Department.

http://www.mpd.gov

News Story 39

Man Dies in Birthday Party Fight

One man died and two people were injured when a birthday party turned violent early this morning, according to Midcity police officials.

A large group of men crashed a gathering of about 150 people in Lemon Hill Park in East Midcity about 11:00 last night. Words were exchanged between the crashers and some of the party attendees.

According to police, one of the party crashers started waving a handgun and threatening to shoot everybody at the party.

People began to leave and a fight broke out in the parking lot of the park. Several shots were fired, according to police.

Officers arrived about 12:45 a.m. and found a man and two women on the ground near the parking lot. The 23-year-old man was dead at the scene. The two women were taken to Midcity Memorial Hospital.

One woman had gunshot wounds to her arm and leg. Her wounds were not considered life-threatening. The other woman suffered a wound to her back, but it was not considered life-threatening.

Witnesses told police that the gunman was between 18 and 22 with a heavy build and a shaved head. Police said they have not discovered a motive for the shootings so far.

The deceased man identified as Darrell C. Houston, 23, 7651-D Canyon View Ct. The names of the two women not released yet.

Police are asking anyone with information about the shooting to call the Midcity Police Department Homicide Unit at (555) 531-9112 or Crime Stoppers at (888) 911-TIPS.

Information obtained from David Cohen, public information officer, MPD.

http://www.mpd.gov

News Story 40

Child Abuse and Family Violence Declines

Professors at Midcity University conducted a secondary analysis of statistics from the Bureau of Justice Statistics and found that child abuse and other forms of violence involving family members fell by more than half in the past ten years.

Professors in the Department of Family Studies and Child Development examined reports to law enforcement agencies in all 50 states and the District of Columbia.

Quote from Dr. Juanita M. Cruz, chairwoman, Department of Family Studies and Child Development, Midcity University:

"The decline in domestic violence is consistent with the decline in crime overall in the past decade. Our findings are encouraging, but there's a lot more work that needs to be done to reduce the number of incidents even more."

The rate of family violence fell from about 5.4 victims to 2.1 victims per 1,000 residents age 12 and older.

Simple assault was the most frequent violent offense and murder was the least frequent offense.

Other findings included the following:

73% of victims were female
75% of offenders were male
74% of victims were white
79% of offenders were white
62% of victims were between the ages of 25 and 54
66% of offenders were 30 or older

Quote from Karen Murphy, director, Midcity Family Violence Prevention Institute:

"The Midcity University report is a real ray of hope that the United States is on the right track in dealing with the type of violence that can devastate families. Our work is not done, though. We still have way too much domestic, dating and family violence. We simply have to do more to protect women and children and provide safe environments for them."

Dr. Cruz was the head of the research team that conducted the study. Other Midcity University professors who participated in the project included:

Dr. Stanley Davis
Dr. Sarah Holtz
Dr. Leslie Chang

All the professors are members of the faculty in the Department of Family Studies and Child Development.

http://www.mufscd.edu
http://www.midcityfamilyviolencegroup.org

News Story 41

Elderly Woman Scammed Out of $5,000

An elderly woman was duped out of $5,000 yesterday by a man and a woman who conned her into believing she was contributing to a charity, according to Midcity police officials.

A woman approached the elderly woman at the Mall of Midcity about 1:00 p.m. yesterday and asked for information about banks in the area. The woman said she was from New Zealand and she wanted to make a large donation to a local charity before she returned to her country at the end of the week. She said she had to provide proof of sufficient funds and was having trouble reaching her bank in New Zealand. She produced a bank book that indicated she had more than $250,000 in her bank.

While the woman was talking to the elderly woman, a man walked up and said he had overheard their conversation. He said he worked at a local bank and would be willing to cash a check for her on the spot. He said he was taking some money from one of the stores in the mall to the bank and had the money on him. When he came up $5,000 short, the woman asked the elderly woman if she would be willing to take a check for $5,000 in exchange for cash so she could complete her promised donation.

The elderly woman agreed and accompanied the pair to her bank, which was located at the south end of the mall. After she withdrew $5,000 from her account, the woman asked her to ask the manager of the bank for a note explaining the transaction. While the elderly woman waited to talk with the manager, the pair ran out of the bank and disappeared into the crowd at the mall.

The woman was described as white, in her 40s, 5-foot-2, heavy build, with short-cropped blonde hair. The man was described as white, in his 50s, 5-foot-10, slender, with dark hair and a mustache.

Anyone with information about the pair is asked to call the Midcity Police Department at (555) 531-9111.

Information obtained from David Cohen, public information officer, MPD.

http://www.mpd.gov

News Story 42

Skateboarder Dies in Traffic Accident

Information obtained from David Cohen, public information officer, Midcity Police Department.

A skateboarder died in a traffic accident this morning.

Accident occurred at 9:47 a.m.

Victim: Gary C. Malcom, 22, 8274 Hudson Court.

Details: Gary Malcom died at 10:19 a.m. today after he fell off his skateboard and was run over by a 2004 Ford Expedition. Gary Malcom was being towed by the Expedition. The Expedition was driven by Paul D. Malcom, 18, 8274 Hudson Court. Paul Malcom is Gary Malcom's brother. The accident occurred at the corner of Lindale Lane and Jefferson Street. Witnesses told investigators that the two men were traveling east on Jefferson Street when the Expedition pulled over to the side of the road. Gary Malcom got out, mounted his skateboard and held onto the passenger side door as Paul Malcom pulled into the street. After traveling about 15 mph for about 500 feet, the Expedition turned sharply onto Lindale Lane. Gary Malcom feel off his skateboard, hit his head on the pavement and was run over by the SUV's rear wheel. Gary Malcom was not wearing a helmet or any other protective gear.

Witness heard Paul Malcom make the following comment after he exited the SUV:

"It was all my fault. It was all my fault."

Sarah J. Holtzman was driving on Jefferson Street with her three children in the car and noticed the stunt.

Quote from Sarah J. Holtzman:

"The first thing I said to my children was 'Look at that guy. He must be crazy. Be sure you never do anything like that. It's an accident waiting to happen.' Then he fell and I saw the SUV roll right over him. It was awful. I pulled over and tried to help. He wasn't moving at all."

Several other bystanders also tried to help. One started CPR and another called 911.

Gary Malcom was taken to Midcity General Hospital, where he was declared dead shortly after his arrival.

Midcity police officers arrested Paul Malcom on suspicion of vehicular manslaughter.

MPD Lt. Thomas Jensen made the arrest.

Quote from Lt. Thomas Jensen:

"It is illegal for a motorist to tow a person on a bike, skates or skateboard. We're continuing our investigation and we might end up filing more charges against Mr. Malcom."

Paul Malcom was taken to jail for processing.

http://www.mpd.gov

News Story 43

Brother of Dead Skateboarder to Warn Others of Dangers

A man who played a role in his brother's death by towing him on a skateboard will not be charged with a crime. Instead, prosecutors will permit Paul Malcom, 18, to spend the next year educating young skateboarders about the dangers of attempting such stunts.

Two months ago, Malcom and his older brother, Gary Malcom, 22, were driving in an SUV on Jefferson Street. The pair pulled to the side of the road and Gary Malcom got out with his skateboard. He grabbed the handle on the door as Paul Malcom pulled away from the curb. When the SUV turned sharply onto Lindale Lane, Gary Malcom fell off his skateboard, hit his head on the pavement and was run over by the SUV's rear wheel. He died soon after his arrival at Midcity General Hospital.

Paul Malcom was arrested on suspicion of vehicular manslaughter.

Instead of being charged with a crime, Paul Malcom will give skateboard safety presentations at local skateboard parks and local elementary, middle and high schools.

Quote from Edward Whittler, district attorney:

"We think the decision not to prosecute Mr. Malcom is in the best interest of justice. I have every confidence that Mr. Malcom will be able to help many other people avoid the kind of heartache that he and his family have suffered."

Whittler made the announcement this morning at a news conference. He said he and members of his office had met with Malcom's attorney, family members and law enforcement officials before deciding to grant Malcom's request to serve as a skateboard safety lecturer.

Quote from Craig Kegel, attorney for Paul Malcom:

"Paul Malcom has devised a comprehensive plan to help other skateboarders understand the dangers associated with skateboarding in traffic lanes. Paul is going to make heart-felt presentations, pass out flyers and show safety videos to cast light on the perils of attempting certain tricks."

Malcom has invited several professional skateboarders to join him in his push to increase awareness of skateboard safety, according to Kegel.

Quote from Marianne Malcom, 47, mother of Paul and Gary Malcom:

"We're relieved that Paul won't have to go to jail. He's suffered so much already. He loved his big brother so much. By getting to warn others about the dangers that go along with skateboarding, it should help him grieve for his brother in a positive way."

Quote from Paul Malcom:

"I hope I'll be able to convince people, especially kids, to stay away from stupid stunts. I miss my brother so much. What we did was so stupid. I think about it every day."

http://www.midcitydistrictattorney.gov
http://www.skateboardingassoc.safety.org

News Story 44

One in Three American Adults Suffer from Insomnia

A conference on insomnia held at Midcity University today. Keynote address featured Dr. James R. Smith, dean, School of Medicine, Midcity University. In his address, Dr. Smith presented the following information:

About 33% of adults in the United States have trouble sleeping.

About 10% of adults in the United States have symptoms of daytime impairment that signal true insomnia. Such symptoms include walking around in a fog, slowed memory and other cognitive functions, dozing off behind the wheel of a vehicle, depressions and a lack of energy.

Self-medicating with any sort of pill or alcohol is a bad idea.

Despite years of study, scientists know very little about what causes chronic insomnia, its health consequences and how best to treat it.

Most experts agree that chronic insomnia is a major public health problem.

There are a great many myths and misinformation associated with chronic insomnia. The most commonly used treatments—alcohol and over-the-counter sedating antihistamines such as Benadryl—are really not very effective. Alcohol actually disrupts quality sleep and antihistamines can cause a variety of problems, including lingering daytime sedation. There is no evidence that popular dietary supplements, including melatonin and valerian, help fight insomnia.

Treatments that do seem to work or that have shown promising potential:

1. Cognitive and/or behavioral therapy. Such therapies can help people reduce their anxieties. Right now, not many health providers are trained in such techniques, however.

2. Newer prescription sleeping pills, including Sonata, Ambien and Lunesta, seem to work well without many of the side-effects of older pills. More research is needed on the new pills to determine their long-term effectiveness, however.

Quote from Dr. James R. Smith, dean, School of Medicine, Midcity University:

"Insomnia is definitely a major public health problem in the United States. We need a broad range of new research into the causes, effects and treatments of insomnia. With such research will surely come new and better treatments. It's important that we act now, though. Statistics show that every year, more American adults report that they are having trouble sleeping."

http://www.mumedicine.edu

News Story 45

Brush Fire Burning in East Midcity

A fire set to destroy brush and dead trees got out of control in East Midcity this morning and has burned 400 acres so far, according to Midcity Fire Department officials.

No injuries reported so far.

No homes destroyed, but several equipment sheds and recreational vehicles have been destroyed.

No evacuations have been ordered, but officials have indicated that evacuations might be in order if the fire is not brought under control in the next several hours.

The fire is burning in a relatively rural area, but it is being pushed toward a new housing development.

About 200 firefighters have been battling the blaze. Two helicopters and two tanker planes are being used as well.

The prescribed burn began about 7:00 a.m. this morning, but unexpected winds kicked up and firefighters lost control.

Quote from Caitlyn S. McFadden, fire captain, Midcity Fire Department:

"We have about 65% containment on the fire now and things look pretty good. The winds have died down and the choppers and tankers are doing a good job. I expect 100% containment by morning."

Information obtained from Kara Portillo, public information officer, Midcity Fire Department.

http://www.mfd.gov

Shot List:

1. Cover shot of fire and firefighters	:06
2. Cover shot of winds whipping trees/bushes	:06
3. Medium shot of a burning shed	:03
4. Medium shot of burned recreational vehicles	:03
5. Close-up of Capt. McFadden	:06
6. Cover shot of housing project with smoke in background	:06
7. Cover shot of helicopter dropping water on flames	:06

News Story 46

Downtown Food Store Gutted by Fire

Information obtained from Kara Portillo, public information officer, Midcity Fire Department.

2-alarm fire gutted a food store in the heart of Midcity's downtown redevelopment district early this morning.

Fire started about 5:30 a.m.

Fire began in a storage room in the rear of "Rusty's Market," 621 Market Street.

Flames had spread throughout the store by the time firefighters arrived 5 minutes later.

The fire destroyed merchandise, equipment and facilities valued at $900,000.

The main structure, a brick building, survived the inferno.

The building was built in 1914.

Quote from Caitlyn S. McFadden, fire captain, Midcity Fire Department:

"We've ruled out any accidental ignition sources, so we believe the fire was intentionally set. We found some gasoline-soaked rags in a dumpster in the alley behind the store. It's likely the arsonist used them to sop up gas from the scene and then just tossed them in the dumpster. We're still investigating, though."

Attempts to contact the owners of "Rusty's Market" have been unsuccessful.

"Rusty's Market" was one of the first refurbished businesses in the heart of the downtown redevelopment district in Midcity. The store stocked mostly culinary specialty items not available in most food supermarkets.

"Rusty's Market" had been in business for almost five years.

Quote from David Cooke, director, Downtown Redevelopment Committee:

"It's never good when you lose a business, but Rusty's was a special place. It was kind of an anchor for us. The great ethnic variety of foods they offered was perfect for what we're trying to do downtown. I sure hope they will be able to reopen."

http://www.mfd.gov
http://www.midcityredevelopgroup.org
http://www.rusty'smarket.com

Shot List:

1. Cover shot of store and firefighters	:06	
2. Medium shot of inside of store	:06	
3. Close-up shot of Capt. McFadden	:06	
4. Medium shot of dumpster and alley	:06	
5. Medium shot of rubble on floor of store	:06	

News Story 47

4 Die in Petroleum Pipeline Blast

Information obtained from Kara Portillo, public information officer, Midcity Fire Department.

4 people were killed and 13 were injured yesterday afternoon after a construction crew struck an underground petroleum pipeline, setting off a huge explosion and fire that burned several buildings and sent flames shooting more than 20 feet into the air.

Peavy Construction Co. performing the work. Peavy is a Midcity-based company that specializes in pipeline work.

The dead have been identified as members of the construction crew that was working on the Midcity Municipal Utility District water pipe replacement project.

Quote from Gregory Moran, foreman, Peavy Construction Co.:

"We had about 10 workers in the trench at the time of the explosion. It's a horrible, horrible thing. We always check with the proper authorities to find out where important power lines and pipelines are located before we start digging. I don't know how this happened. It was supposed to be all clear where we were digging. I'm devastated by this. We're all like family."

The deceased include:

Peter V. Andersen, 52, 1976 Dakota Ave., Midcity
Nancy W. Kline, 36, 738 W. Parkway Dr., Midcity
John K. Enright, 56, 3490 Lemon St., Midcity
Miguel E. Ramirez, 41, 832C Monte Vista Blvd., Midcity

All of the injured people taken to Midcity General Hospital. None of the injured has life-threatening injuries. All listed in satisfactory condition. Most suffered burns or minor contusions, lacerations and abrasions.

60 firefighters were at the scene and had the fire under control within an hour after the 2:30 blast.

The explosion occurred in a mixed residential-commercial area just east of the downtown area of Midcity.

As many as 130 homes, 50 businesses and Clinton High School had to be evacuated.

The fire that followed the blast spread quickly to a nearby apartment building, two single-family homes and retail stores. One of the homes was gutted, but the apartment building, the other home and three retail stores suffered minimal damage.

The ruptured pipe is owned by Dunphy Energy Associates, a Dallas-based distributor of refined petroleum products. The pipe carries gasoline, diesel and jet fuel from a refinery in East Midcity to the Midcity Municipal Airport.

No damage estimate yet.

http://www.mfd.gov
http://www.dunphyenergy.com
http://www.peavyconstruction.com

Picture:

Shows flames engulfing buildings. Firefighters spraying foam on flames. Several fire fighting vehicles visible.

News Story 48

SAT Scores for Local Students Highest in 20 Years

Information obtained from Lisa Ortega, public information officer, Midcity Unified School District.

Midcity students scored better than the national average on the latest round of SAT scores. The SAT is the most recognized college entrance exam.

The average combined verbal and math score for Midcity students was 1,578, the highest score in the past 20 years and a gain of 10 points over last year's average score.

The national average SAT score this year was 1,576.

Quote from Donna Miller Bloomer, superintendent, Midcity Unified School District:

> "We're thrilled. Our teachers, students and parents have worked hard to make this happen. We have more students taking harder math courses and with computers in every classroom now, it's really paying off. In addition, I'm sure the grants we've gotten to provide SAT workshops after school and on weekends helped a lot of students improve their scores."

The average critical reading score increased six points from last year to 505.

The average math score increased four points from last year to 523.

The average writing score increased five points from last year to 550.

The national average critical reading score was 507.

The national average math score was 519.

The national average writing score was 550.

The SAT I evaluates critical reading, math and writing skills. The three tests are each scored on a scale of 200-800.

48% of the nation's 2.94 million high school seniors took the SAT this year.

46% of Midcity's 15,040 high school seniors took the SAT this year.

http://www.musd.edu

Chart:

Set bars of slightly different heights are shown. Three are red and three are blue. Below the three red bars are the words, "National Scores." Below the three blue bars are the words, "Midcity Scores." One of the red bars is labeled "Critical Reading," one is labeled "Math" and one is labeled "Writing." The same labels appear on the blue bars. The number 507 rests on top of the red "Critical Reading" bar. The number 519 rests on top of the red "Math" bar. The number 550 rests on top of the red "Writing" bar. The number 505 rests on top of the blue "Critical Reading" bar. The number 523 rests on top of the blue "Math" bar. The number 550 rests on top of the blue "Writing" bar.

News Story 49

Famous Oak Tree in France Pulled Down

PARIS—The favorite tree of Marie Antoinette, which had stood proudly in the gardens of the Versailles Palace here for more than three centuries, was uprooted and pulled down this morning.

The oak tree died during France's devastating heat wave last summer. The tree stood 66-feet tall and had been planted in 1685.

The tree was known as "Marie Antoinette's Oak." It was a well-known part of the lavish gardens around the Versailles Palace, the extravagant residence of French kings from 1682 until the French revolution in 1789.

Marie Antoinette reportedly enjoyed sitting underneath the tree in the years prior to the revolution that would cost her head in 1793.

The tree will "live" on, in a way. It's 60-ton trunk will be placed in a new location within the gardens and will remain in the gardens as a kind of "work of art," according to a spokesperson for the gardens.

The Versailles Palace is known for its 2,000-acre grounds, fountains, walkways and geometric gardens. It attracts about 9,000,000 visitors each year.

http://www.versaillespalace.com

Picture:

Shows "Marie Antoinette's Oak" in all its robust glory. Picture was taken 3 years ago.

News Story 50

NEWS   NEWS   NEWS   NEWS   NEWS   NEWS   NEWS   NEWS   NEWS

News from Midcity University

For Immediate Release   **For More Information**
                                                                                                1.877.555-MUMU

FAT CATS AND ROUND HOUNDS ABOUND IN U.S.

American pets are looking more like their owners every day. They're overweight.

A study just completed by professors in Midcity University's School of Veterinary Medicine found more than 33% of American dog and cats are overweight.

"One of the problems is owners love to give their pets treats and scraps from the table. It's seen as a sign of affection, but such expressions of love actually contribute to a variety of weight-related problems and even premature death in pets," said Dr. Sophia Mullins, assistant professor of veterinary nutrition, Midcity University.

Just like people, obese pets have a much greater risk of contracting such diseases as diabetes, heart disease and other health problems, according to Dr. Roger Singh, professor of animal science, Midcity University.

A team of researchers from Midcity University's School of Veterinary Medicine surveyed more than 5,000 veterinarians in all 50 states and asked them to report the weights of the dogs and cats they had treated in the past week. In addition, the researchers randomly surveyed 10,000 pet owners and asked them about the weights of their dogs and cats.

Besides the percentage of overweight pets, the researchers found that obesity in pets increases with the age of the pet and obesity occurs more frequently in neutered animals.

"You should be able to feel the ribs of a healthy dog, but if you if you can see the ribs or the pelvic bones of a dog, it is too thin," Dr. Singh said. "For cats, if it looks overweight, it probably is overweight. A normal weight cat has no fat deposits on its back, face or limbs."

Dr. Mullins said pet owners can help their animals trim down by offering them less of their regular food and eliminating table scraps.

For more information on pet health, the researchers recommend that people visit a web site established by the National Research Council.

The web address is http://dels.nas.edu/banr/petdoor.html.

For more information about the research project, visit http://www.muveterinarians.edu.

##########

News Story 51

Construction Worker Loses Eye in Weird Accident

Patrick Howser, 34, 9852 Afton Circle, West Midcity, lost an eye in a construction accident yesterday. He fell off a ladder and fell onto an 18-inch drill bit. The bit poked through his left eye and out the back of his skull.

Howser lost his eye, but suffered no brain damage.

The drill bit was 1.5-inches in diameter.

According to doctors at Midcity Memorial Hospital, the drill bit pushed Howser's brain aside rather than piercing into it. Had the bit pushed into Hower's brain, it likely would have caused major brain damage or death, doctors said.

Howser was drilling above his head when the ladder he was standing on started to wobble. Howser tossed the drill aside, as workers are encouraged to do. When he fell off the ladder, he landed face first onto the drill.

Howser is employed by Lucia & Warner Home Builders. He was working on a townhouse project in North Midcity.

Audio Cut from Patric Howser:

"It's really a miracle, I guess. All the doctors and my co-workers can't believe I survived. I looked like something out of a horror movie with that drill bit sticking out of my skull."

Audio Cut from Patric Howser:

"As I was falling, I could see the drill bit. I felt some pressure as I landed, but no great pain. I ran my hands up the drill bit until I felt my nose and eyebrow. Then I reached to the back of my head and felt the rest of the bit. I knew then that I was in trouble. I guess I should have thrown the drill a bit more to the side."

Audio Cut from Jesus Reyes, Fire Caption, Midcity Fire Department:

"That drill bit sticking through that guy's head was the most bizarre thing I've seen in my 33 years as a firefighter. He took it like a trooper, though. He was a lot calmer than I would have been with a drill bit stuck through my eye."

http://www.mfd.gov
http://www.lucia&warnerhomes.com

News Story 52

Home Mortgage Rates Inch Higher

Information obtained from Alexis North, director, Midcity Realtors Association.

Rates on 30-year, fixed-rate mortgages averaged 6.76% for the week that ended yesterday.

The rate for the previous week was 6.70.

Rates reached a high for the year six months ago at 7.34%. Rates have bounced around since then, but have drifted lower most weeks.

15-year, fixed-rate mortgages, a popular option for people looking to refinance their homes, averaged 6.16% last week.

The rate for 15-year mortgages was 6.08% the previous week.

1-year, adjustable-rate mortgages averaged 5.16% last week.

The rate for 1-year ARMs was 5% the previous week.

The increases, especially on the ARMs, are attributed to the Federal Reserve Board's decision to boost a key short-term rate by 1/4% to 3%.

Announced mortgage rates do not include add-on fees known as points that lenders often charge borrowers.

The average points charged for 30- and 15-year mortgages was 0.7.

The average points charged for 1-year ARMs was 0.6.

One "point" equals 1% of the loan amount.

In addition to points, which can run as high as 2 to 3 on a loan, many lenders pass on "closing costs" to borrows as well. Such costs include escrow fees, title fees, appraisal fees, filing costs, etc. Closing costs can be several thousand dollars on certain loans.

http://www.midcityrealtorsassn.org
http://www.federalreserveboard.gov

News Story 53

Daily Business Report: Stocks Up, Dollar Mixed, Oil Cheaper

Stocks up today.

The Dow Jones industrial average climbed 31.61 (0.31 percent). The Dow finished at 10,302.29. The Dow had fallen 103 points in the first hour of trading.

The Nasdaq composite index rose 7.01 (0.34 percent). The Nasdaq finished at 2,075.66.

The Standard & Poor's 500 index was up 2.93 (0.25 percent). Standard & Poor's finished at 1,197.87.

Advancing issues outnumbered decliners by more than 9 to 7 on the New York Stock Exchange. Volume was 2.01 billion shares.

The yield on the 10-year Treasury note fell to 4.06 from 4.07.

The dollar hit a 15-month high against the British pound, but was down against the Euro. The dollar was mixed against other currencies.

Crude oil prices fell to $57.20 per barrel, down 55 cents from yesterday.

http://www.nyse.org
http://www.moneymatters.com

News Story 54

Woman Has Baby in Bathroom After Hospital Sends Her Home

South Midcity woman gave birth to a boy at 2:45 p.m. today in her home.

Baby was delivered by the woman's husband in the toilet.

Janette L. Calloway, 29, was sent home from Midcity Community Hospital at 12:45 today.

Calloway and her husband, Michael J. Calloway, 31, had spent nearly five hours at the hospital, but were sent home because doctors said she was not ready to deliver.

The baby, Mickey Mantle Calloway, is reported to be healthy and in good condition.

A spokeswoman for Midcity Community Hospital, Susan Wolfe, refused to comment citing federal patient privacy laws.

Soon after arriving at their home, Mrs. Calloway said she felt the need to use the restroom.

Firefighters and paramedics were called, but by the time they arrived, they really weren't needed.

This is the first child for the Calloways.

Audio/Video Cut from Janette Calloway:

"I knew I was ready to have the baby, but the doctors told us to go home. I'm glad things turned out all right, though. My baby's perfect. He's so beautiful."

Audio/Video Cut from Michael Calloway:

"Janette was in the bathroom and I heard her say she thought she was having the baby. I rushed in saw the baby half way into the toilet. I scooped him out, dried him off and let Janette hold him."

Audio/Video Cut From Joseph Leiter, Fire Captain, Midcity Fire Department:

"The Calloways did everything right. We just made sure the baby was breathing properly and we also checked Mrs. Calloway."

http://www.mfd.gov

News Story 55

Lightening Strikes Ignite Local Brush Fires

Approximately 1,500 bolts of lightening struck the Midcity area last night. The strikes ignited four brush fires.

With the area in the midst of a heat wave, fire officials are concerned about additional brush fires in the next several days.

With several rounds of thunderstorms expected the rest of the week, fire officials are preparing for the worst.

Fire officials are particularly concerned about "hold-over" areas, where a lightening strike causes a tree to smolder for a day or two and then suddenly erupts into a major fire.

Fire officials report they plan to fly over the rural parts of the city today in an attempt to spot the "hot" areas and douse them before they ignite.

Lightening strikes were blamed for the following fires:

> 150 acres near Green Valley Road and Wildhorse Canyon Drive.
> 100 acres near Mountain Lion Way and Meadowbrooke Street.
> 200 acres near Hidden Lake Place and Hidden Glen Drive.
> 300 acres near Corral Court and Lookout Lane.

No injuries reported.

No structures damaged.

Firefighters fought all of the fires with helicopters, air tankers, engine companies, bulldozers and fire crews.

All of the fires were contained by 1:00 p.m. today.

Audio/Video Cut From Caitlyn S. Mcfadden, Fire Captain, Midcity Fire Department:

> We had an amazing number of lightening strikes last night. We're actually lucky we didn't have more fires. Things are so dry, it doesn't take much to get a fire started in the brush and grass."

http://www.mfd.gov
http://www.nationalweatherservice.midcity.gov